The Christian
and the Pharisee

£2

The Christian and the Pharisee

Two outspoken religious leaders
debate the road to Heaven

R.T. Kendall
and David Rosen

HODDER &
STOUGHTON

First published in Great Britain in 2006

2

British Library Cataloguing in Publication Data
A record for this book is available from the British Library

ISBN-10: 0 340 90874 2
ISBN-13: 9780340908747

Printed and bound in Great Britain by
Clays Ltd, St Ives plc

The paper and board used in this paperback are natural recyclable
products made from wood grown in sustainable forests.
The manufacturing processes conform to the environmental
regulations of the country of origin.

Hodder & Stoughton
A Division of Hodder Headline Ltd
338 Euston Road
London NW1 3BH
www.madaboutbooks.com
and
www.hodderbibles.co.uk

Dedicated to all who seek the peace of Jerusalem

Contents

Foreword

by Lord George Carey

The relationship between Judaism and Christianity is arguably one of the longest in the history of interfaith and cultural associations. Sadly, it has been, on the whole, a history of bitter misunderstanding and deep conflict. From its earliest days, when Christianity, from within the bowels of Judaism, challenged the central tenets of that faith, the Church has not always acted with kindness and grace towards its older sister. While defenders of the Church will also point out that Judaism must take its share of the blame, there can be no defence of the persecution of Jews through the medieval period up to modern times, resulting in Elie Wiesel's judgment in one of his many books: 'All I know of Christianity,' he writes, 'was its hate for my people.'

It is this background that stands for me as the most extraordinary feature of this timely and amazing book, because *The Christian and the Pharisee* emerges from a deep and very special friendship between an evangelical Christian and leader and a renowned Orthodox rabbi. Both of them I am delighted to call dear friends; indeed, the three of us are actively engaged in resolving the deep divisions between world faiths that scar the religious landscape of our world. R. T. Kendall served with great distinction as pastor of the Westminster Chapel during my time as Archbishop of Canterbury and he graced that venerable pulpit with authoritative preaching and humility. Rabbi David Rosen is one of those remarkable rabbis whose attractive humanity, deep faith and loving attention to people reveal the wonderful luminosity of Judaism.

So, in this book, two great men of faith meet as friends and yet on opposite sides of the divide between Christianity and Judaism. No punches are pulled, no fundamental question of faith is avoided – but with humour, kindness, respect and love, fundamental issues of religion are discussed and probed.

I have not the slightest doubt that this is a book for our times. We live in a polarised world in which people take sides too quickly and in which we are all sucked into old prejudices and rarely given a chance to think for ourselves. Here we are invited into a rich conversation that sets a model for interfaith cooperation and dialogue. This book is required reading for all believers and has the capacity to make a major contribution to healing some of the wounds of history.

George Carey
Lord Carey of Clifton
Archbishop of Canterbury 1991–2002

Foreword
by Chief Rabbi René-Samuel Sirat

Then they who feared the Lord spoke to one another:
and the Lord listened and heard;
and a book of remembrance was written before Him
for those who fear the Lord and take heed of His Name.
And they shall be Mine, said the Lord of hosts
on the day when I pass Judgment
and I shall have compassion on them as a man has compassion
on his son who serves him.

(Malachi 3: 16–17)

The above quotation from the prophet Malachi, last of the Hebrew Biblical Prophets, seems to me a fitting preliminary to this fascinating book of dialogue between a leading preacher, former minister of Westminster Chapel, and one of the most famous rabbis of our time, the former Chief Rabbi of Ireland and an indefatigable representative Jewish voice in inter-religious dialogue.

I don't have the honour of personally knowing the Rev. R.T. Kendall. I hope to meet him in the near future during one of my trips or at an inter-religious meeting but the texts presented here greatly testify to his merit. I can also vouch for the excellence of the speeches, articles, books and debates, through which Chief Rabbi Rosen reflects his remarkable intelligence and deep knowledge of, as well as total devotion to, Judaism.

Since the Seelisberg Conference that took place in 1947 at which the foundations of the Jewish–Christian friendship and cooperation were formulated; and especially since the proclamation *Nostra Aetate* of the Second Vatican Council, the inter-religious dialogue has advanced considerably, thanks to highly talented people like the two coauthors of this book of such an extremely interesting exchange of letters.

However, we must firstly realise that a fundamental asymmetry exists here. Christianity sees its main task to spread everywhere and at all times the idea that Christ brought redemption to humanity. Its calling is therefore essentially to proselytise, whereas Pharisaic Judaism – although it doesn't reject those who seek to convert to Judaism having fallen in love with the God of Israel – and why should it reject them? – still refuses to engage in any kind of proselytism whatsoever. When one approaches the Jewish–Christian dialogue, one should be aware of this main difference between the two religions. It is necessary to explain the reasons for this as formulated by the rabbis. Every man and woman has been created in the Divine image and God in His Supreme wisdom made His creatures part of a particular people, church or congregation, from birth. In order to obtain eternal salvation, he or she who is not born within the Jewish people must observe the laws that (Jewish Tradition teaches) were communicated to our common ancestor, Noah the Patriarch. There are seven such laws and commandments: 1) not to worship idols; 2) not to blaspheme; 3) not to kill; 4) not to steal; 5) not to commit incest or adultery; 6) to submit to the jurisdiction of courts of law (otherwise, life in society would resemble a jungle); and 7) not to eat the flesh of a living animal (which is understood to mean not to cause suffering to animals).

Any non-Jew who observes those commandments – rather like the unconscious expression of Mr Jourdain, in Molière's *Bourgeois Gentilhomme*, merits 'the world to come'. On the other hand, the salvation of a non-Jew who converts to Judaism is actually jeopardised if he or she continues to observe the seven Noahide laws, but fails to keep the laws pertaining to the Sabbath, marital relations, the dietary laws, or the more detailed rules of Jewish ethics. What right would a rabbinic court have to encourage a conversion, unless they were absolutely convinced in all good conscience that the candidate is genuinely willing to become a fully observant Jew?

The greatest scholar of Jewish studies of the last generation – I refer to the famous Rabbi J. B. Soloveitchik, who resided in Boston – was in favour of inter-religious cooperation, but at the same time forbade his followers to take part in any theological debate between Jews and Christians. This was at the very dawning of inter-religious dialogue and he had good reason to be concerned about all possible mishaps. However the situation is not the same today. The friendship between Jews and Christians has known a greater flourishing in the last fifty years than during the previous millennia.

This year we commemorated throughout the whole world and particularly at Troyes in France, his birthplace, the 900th anniversary of the death of Rashi (Rashi is the acronym of Rabbi Shlomo Yitzhaki: 1040–1105). I wish to conclude with the words of this brilliant commentator on the Bible and the Talmud, by quoting his exposition of the verse in Zephaniah (3:9) that appears in his commentary on the Babylonian Talmud treatise Avodah Zarah (24a).

The verse from Zephania reads: 'For then I will restore to the peoples a pure language, that they all may call on the name of the Lord to serve Him with one accord [literally: shoulder to shoulder]' (KJV). Rashi comments: 'That means there will be no more differences between those who serve the Lord. The worship of Israel and the worship of the other nations will be identical and embrace all of God's commandments.'

The dialogue, as represented in this book, brings us closer to this blessed time for which the authors deserve our great and warm thanks accordingly.

Chief Rabbi René-Samuel Sirat
former Chief Rabbi of France and
President of the Conference of European Rabbis

Preface

Pray for the peace of Jerusalem: 'May those who love you be secure. May there be peace within your walls and security within your citadels.' (Ps. 122:6–7)

This book is made up of letters we sent to each other between August 2004 and the early months of 2005. We first met through our involvement with and support for the Alexandria Peace Process, led by the former Archbishop of Canterbury Dr George Carey and Canon Andrew White, his envoy to the Middle East. One may say that this correspondence was born at a Shabbat dinner in Jerusalem. A friendly controversy emerged over a popular caricature of a Pharisee. The Pharisee has not been seen in a very positive light, especially by Christians. It may surprise some that Pharisees were not merely a group that existed two thousand years ago but there are those today who view themselves as the continuation of the Pharasaic tradition, which they believe to be God's revealed moral way of life. Part of the reason for our correspondence was to clarify facts that are not evident from the way Pharisees are depicted in the New Testament.

But the correspondence became more than that. The issues of faith and salvation surfaced and the interchange focused largely not on the road map to peace in the Holy Land but on the way to Heaven. The debate inevitably touched on the issue of Messiah. One of us wasted no time in trying to convince the other why a Jew should acknowledge that Jesus of Nazareth was Israel's promised Messiah. The reply was firm, categorical and consistent – and the reasons for this are clear; the letters speak for themselves.

Some of those who have read our letters have asked, 'Are you still friends?' We can answer: absolutely. More than ever. We hope that this dialogue will serve not only to enlighten the reader about our respective beliefs but will also promote a better understanding between Christians and Jews. We have in common a love for the Hebrew Bible, a conviction that what the Scriptures teach about Israel is true and relevant, and we maintain a strong desire to make peace in the Holy Land. We also have a deep love for Jerusalem. We not only lament the anti-Semitism that is rife in the world but especially condemn it when it has come from those who call themselves Christians.

We express our warm appreciation to our editor David Moloney of Hodder and Stoughton for his wise counsel. We also thank the people there (Martin Mullin, Jean Whitnall, Victoria Bullock and Cecilia Moore) for their help, not to mention our gratitude to Hodder for publishing our correspondence.

We particularly thank Dr George Carey and Rabbi René-Samuel Sirat for their kind Forewords to our book.

RT has requested that some significant news (which came to light only days before this book went to press) be inserted here, that David Rosen has been given a Papal Knighthood. He is the first Knight Commander appointed by Pope Benedict, the first Orthodox Rabbi and the first Israeli to receive the award.

RT would also like to thank a number of friends who have read the correspondence, even if so many of their suggestions came 'too late'. It was felt that we should publish our letters as they were originally written, even if we later saw things we might well have written differently. RT therefore thanks Michael Eaton, J. John, Mark Stibbe, Michael McCrum, David Mitchell, Rob Parsons, Alan Bell, Lyndon Bowring, and his former secretary at Westminster Chapel, Beryl Grogan. Alan Bell and Lyndon Bowring accompanied Andrew White and RT on their first trip into Ramallah – the event that actually led to an involvement with the Alexandria Peace Process. RT also thanks his wife Louise, not only for her wisdom but for allowing him to be away from home and making no fewer than seven trips to Israel since their retirement.

David expresses his special appreciation to Sharon, his wife, partner, advisor and invaluable critic and also to his administrative assistant Avril Promislow for her work and support as well as to Bernd Koschland for his review of the text.

We sincerely pray that our book will encourage and stimulate you. We dedicate it to all who seek the peace of Jerusalem. 'May the Lord bless you and protect you . . . and bestow upon you shalom' (Numbers 6: 24, 26).

David Rosen   R.T. Kendall
www.rabbidavidrosen.net   www.rtkendallministries.com
Jerusalem   Key Largo, Florida
September 2005   September 2005

Introduction

During my twenty-five years as the minister of Westminster Chapel I prayed publicly every week for peace in the Middle East 'and for the peace of Jerusalem'. If ever there was a prayer one could be sure was absolutely right, this was surely it. Who would have thought, when King David urged people to 'pray for the peace of Jerusalem' (Psalm 122:6) three thousand years ago, that such a prayer would possibly be even more relevant today than it was then?

And yet I never dreamed that I myself would be the slightest bit involved in the peace process in the Middle East. But shortly after I retired and moved to America, as a result of being part of a tour of British Christians to the Holy Land in the summer of 2002, thanks to Julia Fisher, I was privileged to meet Canon Andrew White. For years he has been the Archbishop of Canterbury's envoy to the Middle East. In July 2002 Andrew took me into Ramallah to meet the late Yasser Arafat. When Dr George Carey was Archbishop of Canterbury he also became the architect of the Alexandria Peace Process, a plan that was designed to bring the religious dimension into the efforts to make peace. Canon White thought that my being an American evangelical was relevant and hoped I might get on with the Palestinian leader. What would normally be a twenty-minute visit extended to an hour and forty-five minutes. A surprising friendship – entirely theological and spiritual, not political – developed between Yasser Arafat and me. I ended up visiting him five times and was with him only a month or so before he died in the autumn of 2004.

On the day I met with Arafat for the last time I had breakfast at the Mount Zion Hotel in Jerusalem with Rabbi David Rosen, one of the original signers of the Alexandria Peace Declaration. At that breakfast David and I decided we should publish a book together, made up of our letters to each other. This book actually has its origin in an experience we had in Jerusalem in March 2004, and one for which I was not prepared. Rabbi and Mrs Rosen hosted a Shabbat meal on a Friday evening for those of us who had flown to Israel in support of the Alexandria Peace Process, including Lord and Lady Carey, Canon Andrew White, Alan Bell, Dr Richard Land, the Very Reverend James Diamond, Dr Ravi Zacharias and Christopher Long. It was a wonderful evening. That was the first time I met David. He is the Jerusalem-based International Director of Interreligious Affairs of the American Jewish Committee. He was formerly the Chief Rabbi of Ireland and had been the rabbi of the largest Jewish congregation in South Africa. He endeared himself to all of us as he demonstrated with his wife and children what their Sabbath evenings are like. It even brought us to tears. It was the high-water mark of a memorable week that was filled with meeting with various Jewish, Christian and Islamic religious leaders of that part of the world.

But what startled me prior to my getting to know him was the complimentary way he referred to a Pharisee as he explained the meaning of the Shabbat meal. I was stunned at first because nearly all I have known about a Pharisee is not good, and calling one a Pharisee in the Christian community is no compliment. But Rabbi Rosen regards himself as a Pharisee in our day and wears the label as a badge of honour. If most Christians think that Pharisees are cold, I have to tell you that this man, who is truly a modern Pharisee, was very warm. To make sure I wasn't misunderstanding him I asked him if indeed I rightly discerned that he regards himself as a Pharisee. Absolutely, he replied. Soon afterwards he sent an informative email on the matter. This was the first of our correspondence with each other. I had no idea that it would lead to this book.

But it was partly because I was in the process of finishing my book *Out of the Comfort Zone – Is Your God Too Nice?* that a correspondence with Rabbi Rosen was so relevant. Readers of that book may recall that the final two chapters are about Pharisees – and they are not viewed in a very flattering way. I asked David if he would kindly read them – which he graciously did. His reaction and comments became the basis for the present book.

If you have not read *Out of the Comfort Zone – Is Your God Too Nice?* you may wish to turn to the Appendix at the end of this book and read 'The sin Jesus hated most', which is part of one of the two chapters David read. It refers to the self-righteousness exhibited by the Pharisees as depicted in the New Testament. Keep in mind that David also read the chapter called 'Twenty-six reasons you might be a Pharisee', which is not included in the Appendix. You need to know that Rabbi Rosen sees a very important distinction between those Pharisees Jesus is recorded as addressing and Pharisees as they are truly to be understood. He also believes that today's Pharisees' successors among the Jewish people, of whom he is one, bear no resemblance to those described in the New Testament. Not only that; he told me that he would feel much the same as I do towards those Pharisees Jesus is recorded as addressing. This is what precipitated the present book. A lively correspondence followed our initial interchange and what you now hold in your hands are those letters we have written to each other.

Dr RT Kendall

Letter 1

Dear RT

I welcome the opportunity to respond to your writings for a number of reasons. First, friendship requires that we speak our minds sincerely to one another and I know that we can do that in a manner that is sensitive and respectful to each other and our respective faiths. Second, as people of faith we are seekers of truth and thus where we believe that the truth may be tarnished or misconstrued we have an obligation to say so. However, I believe the most import reason for developing this dialogue is our very relationship. I don't mean just you and me, but that the relationship between Jews and Christians is something special – or at least should be. As the Jewish theologian Martin Buber put it, 'we share a book and that's no small thing'. I would even go so far as to say that there is a divine plan and purpose in our very differences, but perhaps it's too early for us to be talking about that. For starters, it is surely enough for us to acknowledge that we both see the Hebrew Bible – that you call the Old Testament – as the revealed Word of God. The very fact that we share such a bond with this text of divine revelation places us in a special relationship with one another and requires not only a level of communication, honesty and love, that tragically has been so lacking down the course of history, but surely behoves us to work together for the values we share. At the heart of these values are, of course, the Ten Commandments, one of which is the prohibition against bearing false testimony. Almost two thousand years of separation between Christians and Jews has tragically led to much pain and suffering. Thank God, most of this is behind us. Nevertheless, some of the effects of the past still remain with us and even continue to lead people, unwittingly, to bear false witness against others. There is, of course, not just one culprit in this sin, but I greatly welcome the opportunity to tell you, your followers and readers, of how I see continued false testimony against my faith and people being maintained among many good Christians today. Let me reiterate that I do not suspect that this is generally intentional (otherwise I wouldn't call them *good* Christians) – and certainly not in your case, as I know your love for the Jewish people is sincere. The source of this false witness lies precisely in the historic break between the early Christians and the Jewish community from which they came, and has been compounded in the course of time. The result is that not only do we know far too little about one another, we often have no idea how each one sees him or herself even in contemporary terms, let alone historical ones.

So the first thing that I think I need to do is to tell you how I see myself and where I come from.

I see myself as part of the people descended from Abraham, Isaac and Jacob (also known as Israel), with whom God made a Covenant that was ratified at Mount Sinai with their descendants, the children of Israel. This Covenant is an expression of God's everlasting commitment to the children of Israel to be an instrument of His purpose, testifying to His presence in the life and history of humanity. This testimony may take different

6

forms, but ideally it should be through living a way of life as 'a kingdom of priests and a holy nation' (Exod. 19:6). To this end the children of Israel were given a 'road map' at Mount Sinai that we call the Torah. Indeed, as important as it was to find their way to the Promised Land, it was far more important to follow the course of religio-ethical living that was revealed to them at Mount Sinai. Ideally they would live this way of life in the Promised Land. In fact, they were told at Sinai that their ability to live securely in the land was precisely contingent upon following this 'road map' of life and that if we failed we would be exiled from it. Nevertheless we were reassured that God would always bring us back again (Lev. 26:44–5).

Jewish tradition maintains that all the teachings in the Torah – that is, the Five Books of Moses also known as the Pentateuch – were revealed at Mount Sinai, not just the Ten Commandments. Most Orthodox Jews like me accept this tradition. Others see the Sinai revelation as having contained an essence from which the other precepts flowed.

However, as anyone who is familiar with the Pentateuch knows, it contains hundreds of commandments – according to Jewish tradition, 613 to be precise. Of course, a large proportion of these relate to the Temple: its construction; the offerings that took place within it; its maintenance and matters of ritual purity connected with its function. In addition many of the commandments are conditional – even being dependent upon failure to fulfil others. For example, the commandment allowing divorce (Deut. 24:1) is of course conditional on the failure of a marriage. Or, more dramatically, the commandment to lighten the load of your enemy's donkey (Exod. 23:5) implies that one has already desecrated another commandment, for if one loved one's neighbour as oneself (Lev. 19:18) one wouldn't have an enemy in the first place – and one could go on and on. In other words, a far smaller number of commandments are practically relevant to the average person's daily life. Nevertheless, for the believing Jew, following these divine directions means living according to God's will and way. These precepts were revealed to us not only for our good, for our life (Deut. 30:15, 16); but through following them we come close to God, to know and love Him (Deut. 6:5, 6; 10:12, 13; 11:22).

However, many of them are communicated in 'shorthand'. For example, we are told to 'remember the Sabbath day to keep it holy' (Exod. 20:8). What does 'holy' actually mean? How do we go about achieving that goal? According to Jewish tradition, when the Almighty revealed His written word to Moses for the children of Israel, the meaning was explained. The explanations and clarifications of the Written Torah are known in Jewish tradition as the Oral Torah. And indeed, the ongoing process of clarifying their application in changing times and conditions is part of its eternal vitality. Religious Jews have traditionally understood that the practice and study of the Written and Oral Torah is the way of life that God requires of them, that this is the source of the joy and beauty in their lives and is the secret of their survival.

Now, RT, I am about to enter the historic context which is the focus of your faith – the Second Temple period two thousand years ago in the land of Abraham, Isaac and Jacob.

Already by then much had happened to the children of Israel. The ten tribes of Israel in the northern part of the land had been conquered by the Assyrians and were lost to the southern tribes, who were known by the name of the dominant tribe, Judah (from which, of course, come the names Judea and Jew). Then Judea was conquered by the Babylonians and Solomon's Temple was destroyed, but the Jews survived the cataclysm. The Persians let us return, the Temple was rebuilt, but then we were subsequently subjugated by the Greeks and then the Romans. The result of all these comings and goings and various cultural influences was that by the time Rome ruled in the Middle East the Jewish nation was more diverse than ever.

Our main historic source for that period of time is Josephus, who describes four primary groups of Jews who were active at the time: Sadducees, Pharisees, Essenes and Zealots.

The Essenes and the Zealots represented different reactions to the effects of oppressive Roman rule. The first of these chose to withdraw from general society, which was seen as corrupt and degenerate, and to prepare themselves for the end of that society, which God would destroy and replace with one in their image. The Zealots believed that what God wanted was for them to take up arms to defeat the pagan Romans, notwithstanding the latter's physical might.

However, the two mainstream groups among the Jewish people were the Sadducees and the Pharisees.

The purpose of all the previous historical retrospective that I have given is to explain to you now how generations of Jews over almost two millennia have viewed these two groups.

As Josephus records, the politically dominant group that was the usual address for the Roman authorities and often served as their surrogate was the Sadducees. They were made up of dominant priestly families who controlled the Temple and wealthy segments of society who felt themselves to be part and parcel of Roman culture as well.

Now, there are scholars who view the Pharisees as having been a separatist group, but our traditional view has been that these were the teachers of Jewish tradition, our rabbis and their followers. We have seen them as the heirs of the prophets of Israel and as those who maintained the devotion not only to the Written but also to the Oral Torah. Indeed, the historic evidence makes it clear that one of the main distinctions between the Pharisees and Sadducees was the attitude towards the Oral Tradition. The Sadducees saw this as unnecessary expansion of the Written Torah, which they took much more literally. But there were many other distinctions – not least of all the overwhelming focus of the Sadducees on the Temple service as the key to God's favour. While the Temple was of course an important institution for the Pharisees, they taught – in keeping with the prophets of Israel – that what is most important is one's personal relationship with God and one's relationship with one's neighbour, wherever one may be. As a result, after the rebellion against Rome by the Zealots, the Roman destruction of the Temple and Jerusalem, and the Roman exile of large segments of the Jewish population, the Sadducees, the Essenes and the Zealots all disappeared. The only group among those to which Josephus refers that could survive political failure, the destruction of the Temple and exile, was the group that nurtured the knowledge and practice of the Written and Oral Tradition, as the divine purpose of Jewish existence *wherever* we lived.

The bottom line is that Jewish tradition for most of the last two thousand years viewed the Pharisees as the rabbis of our heritage: heirs of the prophets and biblical tradition, the teachers of authentic Judaism as enshrined in the Talmud – the religion of the Jews as it has been practised and known until modern times.

Therefore, in the perception of most religious Jews today, to denigrate the Pharisees is in fact to denigrate Judaism.

We now approach the big question regarding Jesus' recorded comments regarding the Pharisees.

The question is even larger because of the overwhelming parallels between Jesus' teaching and that of the Pharisees – the rabbis of the Mishnaic period (the Mishnah is the first written version of the Oral Tradition) contemporaneous with Jesus. They emphasised the paramount principles of love of God and neighbour; the importance of the individual's personal relationship with God; the values of modesty, charity, repentance; the significance of the afterlife; that, as holy as the Sabbath is, when it comes to the preservation of human life it must be transgressed. One could go on and on drawing the parallels between the teachings of the Pharisees and Jesus. In fact, I recall that the German scholars Strack and Billerbeck documented hundreds of parallels in the Mishnah and Talmud to the sayings of Jesus in the book of Matthew alone! Virtually all the sins Jesus is recorded as having chastised the Pharisees for, are condemned by the rabbis (whom we see as the Pharisees) themselves. In fact, the similarities are so great that I find it compelling to believe that Jesus himself was part and parcel of that community.

Some scholars would say that the term 'Pharisee' was used in different ways at different times, and that at Jesus' time it did only apply to a limited particularist group which only later became popular and widespread.

Another interpretation raises the question as to why the Sadducees are hardly referred to in the Gospels, especially as they would have been far more likely to have been the object of Jesus' criticism – controlling the Temple, power, access and resources to the degree they did. The answer, they suggest, lies in the fact that the Gospels were written well after the Sadducees as an identifiable group ceased to function. The very survival of the Pharisees in the form of Rabbinic Judaism led to the use of their name to describe those whom Jesus was criticising, when in fact he was berating other groups that were no longer around or no longer relevant to the religious social reality when the Gospels were written.

However, I would point out something else which appears to me to be more important in resolving this riddle.

When the prophets of Israel chastise the people and say things like 'O Israel, why have you forsaken God?' or 'O Judah, how long will you continue to sin?' they are not for one minute suggesting that they, the prophets, are not part of Israel or Judah.

Because Christianity – especially after the conversion of Constantine – tragically increasingly detached itself from its

Jewish roots, Christians forgot that Jesus was a Jew talking overwhelmingly to Jews – good Jews and bad Jews (and most of them probably in between, like most of us!).

When Jesus criticised Pharisees, he was doing so as a rabbi addressing other rabbis, saying, 'You rabbis are letting the side down! Precisely because you *are* rabbis, you should know better and your sin is worse.'

From my traditional Jewish perspective that views the Pharisees as the teachers of Rabbinic Judaism, Jesus *could not* be criticising *all* Pharisees – especially if he was, as I believe, part of that community. Indeed, to claim that he was addressing *all* Pharisees would not only be incorrect in my opinion, it would also imply that Jesus was judging and stigmatising a whole community, which would surely be in complete contradiction with the most sublime religious moral values that he preached. So I am convinced that Jesus was criticising *some* Pharisees – not *all* Pharisees.

I consider it important for Christians to recognise this, not only because I believe that it cannot be true that Jesus stigmatised a whole community for the sins of some of them, but also because I want Christians to be aware of how we Jews today see ourselves as the continuation of the Pharisaic Tradition, of normative Judaism. That is why I am offended by the pejorative use of the word 'Pharisee', as I would be if someone used the phrase 'to Jew somebody' to mean to swindle someone.

As I have said, the sins and hypocrisy that Jesus exposes in *those* Pharisees are precisely exposed by other Pharisees in our rabbinic literature. One of the criticisms is of a dry legalism that is divorced from the spirit of God's commandments. That, however, does not mean that we think that we can disregard them or even treat them lightly. On the contrary, we believe that our fulfilment of these observances and their study is precisely the way of life God wants us to pursue – the way of life that gives joy, beauty and meaning to our existence. But obviously we have to be in consonance with their spiritual goal and purpose of making us holy. Leviticus chapter 19 opens with the commandment: 'You shall be holy because I the Lord am Holy', and this chapter makes it clear that holiness is not only the discipline that makes us conscious of God's presence, but above all is expressed in the love of God and neighbour that leads us to live with care and compassion for our fellow human beings – all created in the Image of God. Thus arrogance, self-righteousness and disdain for others, jealousy, greed or speaking ill of others, etc., are all considered sinful ways to behave – in fact, considered most *un-Pharisaic* ways to behave.

So all I ask, RT, is that you might consider referring in your writings and sermons to *those* Pharisees or *some* Pharisees whom Jesus criticised, and not tarring us all with the brush of individual sinners by association. Because when all Pharisees are presented as sinners, you bear false witness against me.

Yours
David

Letter 2

Dear David

Thank you for the way in which you opened the first chapter. Your kindness, graciousness and wisdom are like the fruit of the Holy Spirit – the very spirit Jesus implied was absent in those Pharisees he addressed in the Sermon on the Mount (Matthew 5, 6, 7). You have set a very high standard – in courage, content and clarity – in what you have written to me. Your own example, moreover, is the best vindication of your claim that those Pharisees Jesus addressed were not what Pharisees are supposed to be like – then and now. In one sense you have already convinced me! Indeed, I can even envisage some readers thinking to themselves as they read the previous chapter, 'He sounds like a Spirit-filled Christian.' I would have to add that, in the time I have got to know you, you certainly do not seem to me to mirror the kind of person that I have always thought a Pharisee was like. It was probably that factor alone that has brought us together to produce this book.

I fear that there are Christians who, when entering into dialogue with those they do not always see eye to eye with, do not show the loving spirit I sense in you. Let it be said that many Christians can learn from at least one Pharisee that I know!

As you early on shared how you see yourself and where you are coming from, it seemed appropriate that I do this as well.

I am a Gentile Christian – of the reformed wing of the Protestant faith. As you helpfully gave a brief history of the various movements in ancient Judaism – Zealots, Essenes, Sadducees and Pharisees – I thought I would do the same to let you know how I fit into our various streams. You will know that Martin Luther (1483–1546) caused a big upheaval in the Roman Catholic Church in the sixteenth century when his rediscovery of justification by faith alone led him to break with Rome. Apart from his inexcusable anti-Semitic comments, which to this day make Christians blush, I am indebted to Martin Luther, but perhaps more so to John Calvin (1509–64), who came a generation later. Calvin, stressing the inner testimony of the Holy Spirit in the context of the sovereignty of God, made Luther's teaching even clearer. Those who generally follow Calvin would be regarded as reformed, or evangelical (although some who are evangelical may not be happy with all the points of reformed theology).

Your explanation of the differences between Pharisees and Sadducees pretty much rules out the comparison that is sometimes made – that evangelicals are more like the ancient Pharisees, and non-evangelicals (liberals) are like the Sadducees. Since I myself would want to be governed entirely by Scripture and not tradition, perhaps I am more of a Sadducee than I thought! But it is my understanding that Sadducees denied much of what is supernatural (e.g. angels, resurrection) which Pharisees affirmed; so in that sense I guess I am more akin to Pharisees.

It seems suitable in any case that you and I, given our backgrounds and views, engage in this correspondence. You probably already know that the term 'evangelical' is often used generally to describe a conservative theological position – e.g. the infallibility of Scripture; the full deity and humanity of the person of Jesus Christ; the need for all to be saved by trusting only Jesus' death and resurrection; Jesus' second coming; and the Final Judgment of all people.

But evangelical theologians are divided on the issue of Israel. Some say that the Church replaced Israel altogether and that God has no further plans for his ancient people – or the land of Israel. I do not agree with this position, usually called 'replacement theology'. But some go to the other extreme and claim that Jews don't even need to be converted – that God will give them a second chance when Jesus comes. I do not agree with this position either.

I regard myself as an evangelical but also one who has experienced the immediate and direct witness of the Holy Spirit. I trusted Jesus as my Saviour on an Easter Sunday morning – 5 April 1942 – when I was six years old. I entered the preaching and pastoral ministry as a member of the Church of the Nazarene (a denomination that stresses holiness). On 31 October 1955 I experienced what I would call the baptism of the Holy Spirit. On that occasion the person of Jesus became very real to me, a full assurance of my salvation was put in my heart and the knowledge of the Holy Scriptures became paramount. My theology changed considerably. From that day on I sought to be theologically sound along with keeping a warm heart.

I loved what you said about the Book we have in common. I agree with you that the Old Testament is the revealed Word of God. On this we will have no difference of opinion. Sadly, there are scholars in the Christian Church that question the infallibility of Scripture, and particularly denigrate the Old Testament – or perhaps I should say, the God of the Old Testament. We even have those who say, 'I can accept the God of the New Testament but not the God of the Old Testament.'

I disagree. I accept the God of the Old Testament as well as the God of the New Testament as being the same God. I take the view that the Old Testament is God-breathed (2 Tim. 3:16) and that those who wrote it spoke from God as they were carried along by the Holy Spirit (2 Pet. 1:21). I regard the New Testament as equally inspired. By the way, is it appropriate if I refer to God in print as 'Yahweh'? I say that because I know you, as an Orthodox rabbi, do not pronounce his name but use *Adonai* instead. I want to respect your wishes regarding this; please forgive me if I have erred already.

I was even more pleased that you brought up the Ten Commandments. It is only a matter of time before you and I will focus on them and the way Jesus interpreted them to those men he called Pharisees. I was glad you put your finger on the Ninth Commandment – about false testimony. This I see as a reminder that I must be utterly, totally and transparently honest in the way I quote you and answer you, and in the way I quote from the Bible.

I expect to learn a lot from you. You have taught me already. If our readers learn from our dialogue, this will be good, of course; but I myself am eager to learn from you and I will ask you not to let me sweep anything under the carpet when I fail to address an issue you raise. This does not mean, of course, that we are going to agree with each other, but I hope we will be open and frank and not let the other off the hook when it comes to points either of us regard as important.

I would like to comment on your statement 'I know that your love for the Jewish people is sincere.' I don't know what I may have said that led you to believe this, but you are exactly right. I had a head start in thinking along this line. My parents were strong Christians. My pastor in Ashland, Kentucky, where I was brought up, always maintained a holy reverence for Jews and for Israel. We were taught unequivocally that the land of Israel was sacred, that Jews were special for they were God's chosen people. This way of thinking began flowing through my veins at a very early age. I walked to school every day with a girl whose name was Connie Goldberg. At times I envied her because she was Jewish and I wasn't. I never dreamed I would one day be part of a book co-authored by an esteemed Orthodox Jewish rabbi. I feel so honoured, David. You may call this over the top, but it is almost like I am on holy ground.

When I was working on my first degree at Trevecca Nazarene University in Nashville, Tennessee, I spent summers working in Washington, DC. I became fairly well acquainted with Rabbi Abraham Kelner, a well-known Orthodox rabbi in that area. He gave me some of his books. I always wondered why he referred to God as 'G-d'. He and his wife invited me into their home for a meal. I remember one thing they served – a ground beef patty (I think it was that). It was my first kosher meal and I can't say I enjoyed it. Sensing this, Rabbi Kelner brought some ketchup, which I doused on my meat! In the course of the evening, discussing Isaiah 53, he lovingly chided me, 'You would like to convert me, wouldn't you?' I blushed and admitted to my wish. He was very good about it and we kept in touch. He wrote me a most kind letter which closed with words I can never forget: 'May you ever ascend to the Mount of the Lord – to which you raise your eyes.'

If you are right, and I suspect you are, that we know 'far too little about one another', I pray this book will help remedy that. It is my urgent prayer that this book will be read equally by both Christians and Jews and that it will be impossible to tell who derives the greater benefit!

It intrigued me that you referred to the Torah as a 'road map'. President George W. Bush has popularised this phrase as he hoped to bring peace to the Middle East with his own plan. As I write these lines, President Bush's plan has not worked. And I think I know why. For the land to which all this pertains is no ordinary land. It goes back to God's ancient Covenant with Abraham. It is special and God still has a soft spot for it. To achieve peace in such a part of the world requires that one bring God into the picture – something I fear has not been done. For God has given his own 'road map' for peace in the land of Israel.

You mention Leviticus 26:44–5, that God would 'always' bring the people of Israel back again to their land. It is not clear to me whether you think there was a necessary condition implied. So let me ask what seems to me to be a most important question in our dialogue. David, is the promise God gave his ancient people regarding possession of the land unconditional or conditional? If it is unconditional, then the people of Israel will inevitably be brought back to their land regardless of their keeping the ancient Covenant God made with them. If it is conditional, then his Covenant people must keep their promise to obey the Torah before they can *expect* to be brought back. Please tell me if it is fair and appropriate to raise this.

Let me return to the issue of the Pharisees. You refer to the matter of divorce. You will know that it is recorded that some Pharisees asked Jesus, 'Is it lawful for a man to divorce his wife for any and every reason?' (Matt. 19:3). I was taught in seminary that there were two schools of thought on this in the ancient rabbinic community: (1) the Hillel school position, that you could divorce your wife simply because you didn't like the way she cooked your supper; (2) the Shammai school, which held that divorce was granted only in the case of adultery. You said divorce was granted on the basis of 'failure of a marriage'. Does this put you somewhere between the two schools? Who or what determines if a marriage has failed? Jesus made it clear in any case that he was unhappy with divorce, that Moses granted it because of their hearts being hard (v. 8). Would you agree with Jesus on this?

I note your phrase 'the believing Jew'. I am interested as to what you mean by that. In what does belief consist? What if a Jew does not believe? How serious is it?

Could I also ask you to say more about the Written Torah vis-à-vis the Oral Torah? Are you absolutely sure that they do not contradict each other? You probably know that a watershed in church history was the Council of Trent (1545) when the Roman Catholic Church decided that tradition was equal with Scripture. This gave a lot of stuff canonical reliability – like the Virgin Mary ascending to Heaven, the Eucharist becoming literally the body of Jesus and the blood of Jesus, or the popes having infallibility when they speak 'ex cathedra'. I therefore know for sure that tradition in church history often goes against Scripture. I am wondering whether you have the same problem in your ancient history. I ask this because Jesus, when addressing a group of Pharisees, is recorded as saying they nullified the Word of God for the sake of their tradition (Matt. 15:6). He also would introduce a thought with the words, 'You have heard that it was said' (Matt. 5:21, 27, 31, 33, 38, 43), when in fact he sometimes refers to the Written Torah and sometimes to tradition. In these references he is recorded as addressing Pharisees – at least, some of them.

I have no doubt that there were good and genuine Pharisees – unlike those Jesus is recorded as addressing. And some of them – of which sort I have no idea – eventually became believers in Jesus. So I agree with you that we Christians, certainly many of us, including me, have erred – even stigmatising you – by painting all of you with a brush that does not allow for a valid distinction among you. So I apologise. I am learning from you. So I take your point: there were those Pharisees Jesus is recorded as having criticised but not all of them were like the ones he spoke against.

But you have opened another subject: what is a sinner? Because you imply that Pharisees are not sinners. Really? David, I myself am a sinner. It does not necessarily mean that I have broken any of the first nine of the Ten Commandments. I don't think it is all that hard to keep the *letter* of the first nine commandments. But what about the Tenth Commandment – 'You shall not covet'? That one convicts me! And it is my understanding of Jesus' teaching in the Sermon on the Mount, when he addressed certain Pharisees, that he always had the Tenth Commandment in mind, even when he quoted any of the other nine. That is why he interpreted the Law and unveiled sin as he did.

I would have little trouble believing the idea you put forward that Jesus himself may have been a part – to say part and parcel calls for too much speculation – of the Pharisaical community in his day. If so, he obviously knew it backwards and forwards. But this may also have given him a greater authority to speak as he did, as you indicated when you referred to the prophets who criticised their own nation. Jesus certainly could have been doing this, especially if his association with them was well known by them and also his hearers. We all get away with criticising far more easily when we criticise ourselves as opposed to criticising another community. By the way, you said that Sadducees are hardly mentioned in the New Testament. That is not quite accurate. And it is speculative to imply a late date on that basis for the writing of the Gospels. Pharisees are mentioned a hundred times, Sadducees fourteen times. Sometimes, however, Jesus lumped them together (Matt. 16:6, 11).

I note your comment that if one loved one's neighbour as oneself one wouldn't have an enemy in the first place. I know what you mean by that. I would only point out that Israel has more enemies than anybody – and has done nothing to cause it. People hate Israel and Jews, but not because of anything they have done – even if an anti-Semitic person brings up their rejection of Jesus as Messiah. The world hates Israel, in my opinion, because Jews are God's ancient chosen Covenant people. Christians, therefore, should be at the head of the queue in esteeming Jews.

I would bring this part of my response to a conclusion by saying that the issue at the end of the day is: what is sin? This is what Jesus was after. He interpreted the Law in a manner that made all of us see that we have not kept the Law but are, indeed, sinners. Those Pharisees he is recorded as addressing apparently had no concept of inward sin but only what is outward – murdering, committing adultery or giving false testimony. If, however, you tell me that you have a conviction of sin as being inward, as your letter to me allowed for (you mention jealousy and greed), then I am compelled to say you are not like the Pharisees Jesus addressed.

Yours
RT

Letter 3

Dear RT

I am already enjoying our correspondence to the degree that I am setting aside other things I should be doing in order to respond as soon as possible.

Before addressing your more substantive points, let me respond to your more 'technical' questions.

Judaism does indeed teach us to revere God's Name (in keeping with the prohibition not to take it in vain, Exodus 20:7) and as a result observant Jews do not articulate the Tetragrammaton – the name made up of the four Hebrew letters YHWH – even in the liturgical reading from the Torah (which takes place every Sabbath morning in an annual cycle; the first part of the forthcoming weekly Torah portion is also read at weekday morning prayers on Mondays and Thursdays and at Saturday afternoon services). In its place, as you correctly mentioned, we use the Hebrew word *Adonai*, which means 'my Lord'. Yet as this word itself has acquired a kind of sanctity, observant Jews do not use it in conversation and tend to use other designations, such as *HaShem* (the Name), *Hakadosh Baruch Hu* (The Holy One Blessed Be He), *Ribono shel Olam*

(Master of the Universe), *Avinu Shebashamayim* (Our Father in Heaven) and many other terms.

In fact, there are other names of God whose common use is frowned upon and which are specified in Maimonides' Code of Jewish Law (based on the Talmud, the compendium of the Oral Tradition based on the Written Tradition). But all of this applies to these names in Hebrew! The practice of writing G-d instead of God has become very commonplace among religious Jews, but it is in fact quite unnecessary and even a little ridiculous, because where will it end? Alm-ghty instead of Almighty? F-ther instead of Father? Sav-r of the Un-vrs-? Taking an important principle (of respect for God's Name) to such unnecessary minutiae might have been precisely the sort of thing that Jesus disliked in those Pharisees he criticised. But as you see, I, who view myself an heir of the Pharisaic tradition, am myself dismissive of such a practice that takes an important principle to unnecessary extremes.

At any rate, RT, you may refer to God as you please and I will not be offended, for I know that however you are referring to Him, your intention is to do so respectfully – and that is the essential thing!

I find it difficult to understand Christians (to whom you refer) who distinguish between 'the God of the Old Testament' and 'the God of the New Testament'. It puzzles me first of all because there is surely only one God! If they were to say 'the way God is portrayed in the Old Testament' at least I could understand it, even if I would disagree with it. God is portrayed in many different ways in the Bible and all of them must be anthropomorphisms, as we mortals can never understand God's essence (that's how Maimonides understands the meaning of Exodus 33:20). As the sages of the Talmud declare, 'The Torah uses language that ordinary human beings can understand.'

However, it seems to me that those Christians who make the above-mentioned distinction are guilty in Christian terms of the heresy of Marcion (of the second century CE) of trying to separate the Hebrew Bible from the New Testament. It would appear that even though this approach was condemned by the Church as a heresy, it is still alive, strong and kicking.

Parallel to this, I am of course aware of the supercessionist teaching that the Church had replaced the Jewish people in God's design (an idea that the Catholic Church formally rejected in 1965 with the promulgation of the document *Nostra Aetate*, which came out of the Second Vatican Ecumenical Council). I am surprised, however, to hear from you that there are evangelical Christians — whom I assume are well versed in Scripture — who would hold to such a view. Aside from the Hebrew Bible's affirmation of the eternity of the Covenant (to which I referred in my first letter to you and refer to below), doesn't Paul confirm this in Romans chapter 11?

This leads us on to the subject of chosenness and the nature of the Covenant that you raise.

Let me state categorically that chosenness implies no inherent superiority — perhaps the contrary (see Deut. 7:7). The Covenant in fact places special obligations, responsibilities and consequences upon the children of Israel. These expectations are not easy to fulfil, and precisely because the expectations are higher, the consequences of failure are greater. (See Lev. 18:25, 26; Amos 3:2.) It is in this light (or rather, shadow) that we have traditionally understood the reason for the destruction of our two Temples and our subsequent exiles. We continue to recite in our festival liturgy:'Because of our sins, we were exiled from our Land.' Naturally, we know that the Babylonians and the Romans were militarily stronger than us and defeated us; but we believed that if we had been fully true to God's Word, Way and Will, the outcome would have been different.

There is, of course, a recognition here of conditionality, but the consequences of this relate to the condition (excuse the pun) of the Jewish people. If they observe God's commandments then they will live securely in the land; if they do not – they will be exiled. In this regard the Covenant is conditional. However, in as much as the children of Israel have been chosen to testify to God's presence in the world (cf. Isaiah 43:10), God's commitment to the Covenant is unconditional and eternal, and thus even after exile the Jewish people will always be given another chance (Lev. 26:44). Moreover, our rabbis teach that even in its very history of exile, the Jewish nation testifies to God's presence through its survival against all odds which is made possible only through God's unlimited love and compassion (Babylonian Talmud (TB) Yoma 69a).

I naturally rejoice in the knowledge that there are many good Christians like yourself who, being profoundly rooted in the Bible, care deeply about the Jewish people – especially those living in the land that the Bible indicates was divinely ordained as the homeland for the children of Israel. I know, of course, that there are many evangelical Christians who support the state of Israel and the ingathering of Jews from around the world within its borders, because they see this as facilitating Jesus' Second Coming. It is not this belief that disturbs me, but rather some of the things this belief leads many of them to advocate and support. Often it leads to politically militant positions opposing any possibility of a territorial compromise with the Palestinians, condemning us to perpetual conflict (these Christians are willing to support a battle to the last Israeli!). Moreover, the above-mentioned conditionality of the Covenant precisely requires the children of Israel to behave with respect, care and compassion for all human beings – all created in the Image of God. Our failure to do so – our failure to live in accordance with the divine commandments – prevents us from being able to live securely in the land, no less than the hostility of our assailants. All this means that we have an obligation to find a solution to the conflict that also respects Palestinians' personal and collective dignity – as well as our own. Christians who love and care for us should feel the imperative to care for the well-being of Palestinians as well. Only when there is security and dignity of both Israelis and Palestinians will we live in the land in peace. I sometimes have the feeling that the eschatological focus on the meaning of Israel blinds some evangelicals to the human realities and needs of the peoples living here!

However, I agree with you that peace in the Middle East will not be achieved if the religious dimension is not there. Precisely for that reason we worked on the Alexandria summit and declaration of religious leaders of the Holy Land from the three Abrahamic faiths. There is much more that I could say on this and generally on the situation in the Holy Land, but I want to return to the theme of Covenant and the questions you raised in relation to it.

Already at the time of the ratification of the Covenant at Sinai and thereafter, there was much sinning amidst the children of Israel (out of either ignorance or weakness). We have always had different kinds of Jews, from the best to the worst (a wit once said, 'Jews are like everyone else, except more so!'). However, the very fact that the Covenant was made with the children of Israel as a whole in perpetuity (see Deut. 29:14) means that it is something of a Catch-22. Once a person is part of the Jewish people, he/she is stuck in it and we are stuck with him/her! Yes, an individual can apostatise, run away, avoid all contact with other Jews, but as the Talmud teaches (TB Sanhedrin 44a), 'Even if a Jew is a sinner, he remains a Jew.' The idea of 'unbelief' is, of course, very much a modern secular concept and there are Jews who do not believe, just as there are non-Jews who do not believe. However, their lack of belief does not mean that they are no longer part of the People of the Covenant, nor that we are discharged from our brotherly responsibilities towards them.

An additional very important point to make here is that

'belief' for Judaism is not what it is for Christianity. In fact, there is a profound distinction here between us. There is no explicit commandment in the Torah to believe in God. Even though Maimonides understood this to be the first of the Ten Commandments, most of our rabbis have seen that first sentence to be simply a statement of fact. God is the reality behind and within the creation and history. To deny that is as sensible as denying that grass is green, which will not stop it growing the same way, or cows from eating it the same way.

Of course, belief is important in Judaism, because that will lead you to live the godly way of life revealed in the Torah. But there's the rub: the purpose, for Judaism, is the way you behave and conduct your life. The purpose is not belief in and of itself. The idea that there is some redeeming power in belief itself is foreign to normative Judaism. (I say 'normative Judaism', because we have produced sects from time to time, like the Sabbateans in the seventeenth century, who did make claim to a redeeming belief.) In fact, if Judaism has to choose between someone believing but not doing and someone doing but not believing, it prefers the latter. The 'sinners' for Judaism are above all those who do not live in accordance with God's commandments.

Now we come to another distinction between Judaism and Christianity. Judaism sees us as sinning because we have free will. Having the power to choose means that we inevitably will make wrong choices here or there, some more often than others. We might do so out of ignorance, weakness, peer pressure, etc., but we do not make the wrong choice (sin) because we are inherently sinful. In fact, Judaism teaches that human beings are basically good; and although we may be weak and easily seduced, unless we are 'damaged' in some way by traumatic experiences, all things being equal, we will prefer to choose good rather than evil. Moreover, as Ecclesiastes puts it (7:20), 'there is not a man who does only good and not sin' (we might better translate it, 'there cannot be a man who does only good and never sins'). Judaism teaches that God has given the answer to this inevitable problem in the concept of *Teshuvah*, inadequately translated as 'repentance'. Actually the word comes from the Hebrew root *shuv*, meaning to return – to return to God and His right path. All of us, Judaism teaches, have within us this capacity for spiritual return and rehabilitation. All we have to do is be sincerely contrite for our specific misdeeds and resolve never to repeat them, and God accepts our sincere contrition unconditionally out of His unlimited love and compassion.

Finally, let me respond to your questions regarding the Oral Torah.

In addition to that which was revealed at Mount Sinai together with the Written Torah, the Oral Torah is also the ongoing exposition and application of the tradition in relation to changing circumstances. This process, in which learned rabbis base themselves on earlier principles and rulings to provide direction on current issues (new subjects today would be things like artificial insemination, heart transplants, stem cell research, etc., etc.), is perceived by Jewish tradition to be guided by the 'Holy Spirit'. Obviously the Oral Tradition would not seek to abolish any principle in the Written Torah. However, there are examples of where the Oral Tradition rendered certain biblical injunctions inapplicable. One obvious example would be slavery. It is clear that the Bible permits slavery even though it does appear to disapprove of it (Exod. 21:2–6). However, the Oral Tradition makes such demands upon slave owners that the Talmud declares that 'He who has a slave has acquired a master over himself.' The result was the *de facto* elimination of slavery.

Another example relates to capital punishment. The Oral Tradition extends the laws of evidence in capital cases so that not only are two witnesses required to corroborate direct visual testimony of a crime before the perpetrator can be convicted for capital punishment (see Deut. 19:15), but two witnesses are also required to confirm that the perpetrator was warned of the consequence of his actions before performing them. To all practical intents and purposes, these requirements overwhelmingly eliminated capital punishment (and required some form of imprisonment in its place). This was obviously motivated by a concern to avoid any miscarriage of justice and out of reverence for human life.

Another example was Hillel's *prosbul*. The Torah declares that the Sabbatical year annuls all outstanding loans (Deut. 15:2). This injunction was given in an agrarian society where money was not a commodity. The purpose of a loan was to enable a farmer who had had a disastrous harvest to purchase new grain to sow for the following year. If he continued to experience difficulties, he would not be able to pay the loan back and could be caught in a poverty trap. Therefore the Sabbatical year was designed, inter alia, to deliver people from such circumstances. However, by the second century BCE, society had become commercial as well and loans were an integral part of economic life. But the cancellation of debts in the Sabbatical year meant that wealthier citizens were holding back on loans as the Sabbatical year approached in case they didn't get their money back, despite the biblical prohibition against doing so (Deut. 15:9). As a result, an injunction that was designed to assist the weak and poor, in a changed socio-economic context was now working against those it sought to help. In order to maintain the spirit of the Law which was now being undermined by the letter of the Law, Hillel introduced a document (known as a '*prosbul*') which basically placed loans in the hands of the courts in order to avoid their cancellation in the Sabbatical year. *De facto*, Hillel abolished this law, although he did so in a manner that maintained the institution *de jure* –

all in order to guarantee the implementation of the spirit and purpose of the Law as the higher goal.

I would see this as having much in common with Jesus' own approach. Accordingly I would explain a criticism of those who nullified the Word of God for the sake of their tradition to be a criticism of those who precisely insisted on maintaining the literal tradition in the text at the expense of the Word of God – meaning its spirit and purpose.

However, Jesus' words as quoted in Matthew to which you refer, 'You have heard it said, love your neighbour and hate your enemy', have always perplexed me, as there is no such phrase in the Written or Oral Torah. Perhaps the Sadducees said this, or perhaps again the writers of the Gospels did not recall Jesus' words correctly. Judaism teaches that we should hate 'evil', not people, i.e. the evil within malfeasant people, but not their being – on the contrary.

In keeping with this, let me clarify that when I commented in my previous letter that if one observed God's commandments one should not have any enemies, I did not mean that the righteous could be guaranteed that no one would hate them. I meant that a righteous person should not regard another as an enemy. If someone hates us because of our ethnic character, colour, etc., etc., that is of course their moral problem. While we must do everything necessary to defend ourselves from such hostility, we have to always try to bear in mind that even one who hates us is still created in the Image of God.

As far as divorce is concerned, the rabbis ruled – where there are differences of opinion among the rabbis, the majority holds sway – in accordance with Hillel, that one did not need an accusation of adultery in order to facilitate divorce. However, Jewish tradition has always frowned upon leniency in this regard and the Rabbinic Courts will always try to facilitate reconciliation and encourage the partners to try to mend the relationship. The process of writing the bill of divorce is complicated and is precisely designed – *inter alia* – to provide time for reconsideration. Certainly divorce reflects a failure and is something to weep over. However – again because we are not perfect creatures and, moreover, because sometimes people who are joined together in marriage may not be successfully suited to one another and may even begin to dislike one another – it is better for them, and generally for their children as well, that they go their separate ways rather than living in conflict under the same roof.

I would agree that any breakdown in human relationships – especially between husband and wife – reflects a hardness of heart somewhere. But we should refrain from pointing an accusing finger. Here we are surely in profound agreement. Jesus says, 'Judge not that you not be judged'; and Hillel the Pharisee, who lived in the century before him, taught 'Never judge your fellow until you are in his place' (Ethics of the Fathers 2:4); and as no one can ever be exactly in another's place, our sages teach us to avoid all self-righteousness and always strive to view others in a generous and magnanimous spirit.

Yours
David

34

Letter 4

Dear David

I was pleased to read that you are enjoying our correspondence. For you to say that you are setting aside other things you ought to be doing shows not only that you are enjoying these interchanges but that they are important to you. Knowing how busy you are, I am amazed how quickly you answered my last letter. But I am reminded of something my father used to say to me, 'If you want to get something done, ask a busy person to do it.'

You have to be the most unusual Pharisee I ever expect to meet! Whether you are considered atypical by your peers, I of course don't know. I was also fascinated by your gracious spirit towards Palestinians. I realise we were introduced to each other by Canon Andrew White, the architect of the Alexandria Peace Process, the religious tract for peace in the Middle East, so I should not have been surprised. But I suspect many evangelicals – perhaps I should call them Fundamentalists, certainly in America – would not expect an Orthodox Jewish rabbi to say that we should feel the imperative to care for the well-being of Palestinians as well as Israeli Jews. I fear that you are right that some of my fellow American Christians, owing to a narrow eschatological focus, don't want Israel to give an inch – for any reason – to Palestinians. Isn't it sad when our theology blinds us to the obvious – our ethical and moral responsibility?

I am thinking I should have defined Fundamentalists in my previous letter. Doing this is not easy since there are several kinds. But, generally speaking, Fundamentalists are seen as rather narrow evangelicals, holding to a brittle theological perspective that embraces an entrenched eschatology: the Second Coming of Jesus before his 1,000-year reign, the restoration of the land to Israel – including the ancient city of Jerusalem (some would throw in the rebuilding of the Temple) – and the conversion of Jews *after* the Second Coming.

But they lead the way in America as being 'friends of Israel'! But, and I think you might agree, they must be more interested in the vindication of their eschatology than they are in easing the pain of suffering people in the meantime. And yet, and I suspect you will agree on this as well, some Fundamentalists remind me of those Pharisees described in Jesus' day who, rather than rejoice that a man was healed, could only lament that it was done on the Sabbath (John 9)! You put your finger on a sensitive but salient point.

You seem surprised that an evangelical could believe in replacement theology. I have to tell you, many if not most of the evangelicals I know accept the view that the Church has replaced Israel in God's scheme. Some prefer a different term, 'fulfilment' theology, by which they mean that the Church has fulfilled the role Israel once had. And they base it on the very chapter you refer to – Romans 11. Largely because Paul said, 'and so all Israel will be saved' (v. 26), they assume he must have meant the entire Church – the complete company of God's elect. Otherwise it would mean that every single Jew without exception will be inevitably and ultimately saved – a view, as I said, that some Fundamentalists actually embrace. Some of these

Fundamentalists do not believe it is necessary to evangelise the Jews because they will get a second chance in any case after the Second Coming. It is then when all Jews who have not been converted to Jesus will finally believe that Jesus is their Messiah. As to those Jews who were deceased, they too will be raised from the dead after the Second Coming and given a second chance to believe in Jesus – which they would certainly do under such circumstances.

But the evangelicals that I know don't believe that at all. They believe, as I do, that Jews must receive Jesus Christ as their Messiah *before* the Second Coming – or they will perish just like anybody else. In other words, many evangelicals see Israel as the 'called out' (cf. Greek *ekklesia*) – those who are effectually called by the Holy Spirit. That way all Israel, all the called out, God's elect, will be saved.

As for Romans 11, this has as much to do with you as it does with me. David, you were born to privilege, if I may put it that way; you are called the natural olive tree by the Apostle Paul in Romans 11, while I, being a Gentile, am called a wild olive shoot that has been grafted in (v. 17). So, thanks be to God, I am now privileged in the end! But I don't deserve this mercy. And Paul tells me never to forget it!

In the meantime, God has not abandoned or replaced the natural olive tree. Far from it; Jews are 'loved on account of the patriarchs' (v. 28) – proof to me that replacement theology comes short of Paul's point in Romans 11. The patriarchs can only mean Abraham, Isaac and Jacob. God still has, as he has always had, a special love for Israel. Paul claims that the Jews were not able to accept their Messiah because of a blindness (Greek *porsis*, 'hardening') – at least in part, because not all Jews rejected Jesus (Paul being a proof of that). I will tell you also that it is my view that there will be a lifting of the blindness that is on Israel, speaking generally, and that they will come in massive numbers to see their true Messiah – Jesus Christ –

before the Second Coming. As to 'all' of Israel being saved, I admit this is a difficult verse. I simply take it that all the elect from within the natural olive tree will eventually come to embrace their Messiah. I say this because Paul earlier stated that 'not all who are descended from Israel are Israel' (Rom. 9:6).

On the other hand, I note that you hold that 'the Jewish people will always be given another chance', by which you mean another chance to be restored to the land. And although you certainly do not believe that Jesus is the true Messiah, you would presumably say that, if he really is the true Messiah, you will be given a second chance at some stage to acknowledge him. Please correct me if I have put words in your mouth! I am not meaning to be unfair, I am only surmising that you – if necessary – would be attracted to the Fundamentalists' view that God will let you have a second chance to believe in Jesus after the Second Coming.

One thing I have not understood is where Orthodox Jews stand with regard to Zionism. I have been told that some Orthodox Jews are anti-Zionists, something I have never understood unless it is because Zionism had a rather secular, non-religious beginning in the middle of the nineteenth century. So, David, are you a Zionist? If not, why not? Many Christians believe that the return of so many Jews to their ancient land is a part of God's providence and eternal plan. As you are cognisant of the Palestinians' plight, how far are you willing to go with regard to the walled city of Jerusalem, including the Temple Mount? Do you envisage a day when the Temple will be rebuilt – on the Temple Mount? Incidentally, when I was at seminary I wrote a monograph entitled 'The Messianic Hope of Modern Israel', so this subject really interests me and I look forward to knowing your own views.

I loved what you said about the matter of being chosen, that it has nothing to do with how deserving one is. My favourite verse in this connection is Exodus 33:19: 'I will have mercy on whom I will have mercy, and I will have compassion on whom I will have compassion.' We both apparently have in common a robust doctrine of election, that God makes the choice. No intelligent reader of the Bible can deny that God chose ancient Israel. But some good people disagree on whether God chose individuals, including Gentiles, in his eternal plan. I believe he did. And, again, the choice is not based on our being deserving. Indeed, Paul said that we have been called not because of anything we have done but because of his own purpose and grace, then adding that the choice was made 'before the beginning of time' (2 Tim. 1:9).

I am, however, puzzled by your comments regarding belief. You even say on this that 'there is a profound distinction between us'. First, I would have thought that 'Hear, O Israel; the LORD our God is one LORD' (Deut. 6:4, KJV) is a fairly strong affirmation of belief, quite apart from the First Commandment. Second, Abraham's belief in God's promise to him is what counted for righteousness (Gen. 15:6). Third, Habakkuk's statement that the righteous shall live by his (God's) faithfulness (Hab. 2:4) is surely based on one's belief in God. Fourth, what is 'trust' (in the Psalms, *passim*) if not belief, or reliance, on God? Surely, however important godly behaviour and conduct is, you cannot put the cart before the horse; what you believe is what leads to what you do. If I have understood you correctly, you are quite right – there is indeed a profound distinction between us when you say that 'redeeming power in belief itself is foreign to normative Judaism'.

You also say that there are Jews who do not believe but their lack of belief does not mean that they are no longer part of the People of the Covenant. But is there no penalty for such unbelief – even if the idea of unbelief is a modern secular concept? Do they not forfeit anything by not believing? Also, is this what you mean by the term 'observant' Jews and 'religious' Jews – as opposed to Jews who do not believe? If you say they are not discharged from their brotherly responsibility, what if they live as though there were no law? Is this not antinomianism? Surely you are not saying that merely being a Jew makes everything all right. You will know that the New Testament assumes two Israels: ethnic Israel, by being born into a Jewish family and being circumcised, and true, or spiritual, Israel – those who have believed. This is what is meant by the verse quoted above, 'Not all who are descended from Israel are Israel' (Rom. 9:6).

This leads me to ask: is Moses more important to you than Abraham? You know that Abraham came some 400 years before Moses. And since the Covenant with Abraham – which was ratified by his faith – was in operation when the Law was given, this means that belief is prior to behaviour. David, please tell me where I am going wrong here.

As to the further distinction you make between Judaism and Christianity – the issue of sin and free will – are you saying that every person born into the world is essentially the same as Adam and Eve *before* their sin in the Garden of Eden? We know they were created with free will – of course. But were not their offspring affected by their sin? So, yes, I agree – this is quite a major distinction between us. Would I be right in summarising our difference at this point as that you say a person is a sinner because he sins, while I say he sins because he was already a sinner? He is innately a sinner, in my opinion, because his heart was prone to sin from birth. Is this not a good translation from the Hebrew: 'Surely I was sinful at birth, sinful from the time my mother conceived me' (Ps. 51:5)? The ancient prophet said that the heart is deceitful above all things and desperately (or incurably) wicked (Jer. 17:9). Please correct me here too if I have got it wrong.

Thank you for clarifying the matter of God being spelled G-d by some. You even say that some in your own circles go to unnecessary extremes in the way they avoid misusing the Name of God and that such might have been precisely the sort of thing that Jesus disliked in those Pharisees he criticised. You amaze me by your honesty and candour. I have long suspected that many Christians have not grasped the meaning of Jesus' interpretation of the Third Commandment (Matt. 5:33–7). Many of us can only think of this command as being a prohibition against cursing by using God's Name when they are angry. Of course God is against that. But the truth is, Jesus spoke against using God's Name for the purpose of promoting one's personal interest – for any reason. Whereas Jesus was not speaking against swearing an oath in a court of law (as some surmise), he warned against misusing God's Name by swearing: if I were to say, for example, 'I call Heaven and earth to witness that God is on my side,' or 'I swear to you in the Name of God that he has told me my eschatology is infallible,' I have abused his Name. It is the worst kind of 'name-dropping'. But most Christians have not grasped this; they only think they are free of abusing the Third Commandment as long as they don't say things like 'Oh my God'. That is only a small part of abusing his Name. So if I am understanding what you say about some of your people – who supposedly feel they are doing their duty in fulfilling the Third Commandment by the way they spell God – so too are there Christians who have their own way of feeling they are not violating the Third Commandment (when in fact they are). I am wondering if you have given much thought to Jesus' way of applying the Third Commandment.

I too have wondered about Jesus' words when he said, 'You have heard that it was said, "Love your neighbour and hate your enemy"' (Matt. 5:43). However, even though this is not a quote from the Torah, could there not have been a consensus after hundreds of years – through an unofficial oral tradition – that led to people commonly saying that? So although there is

41

no explicit command to love your neighbour and hate your enemy, this was the way a good number of ancient people must have thought. In the Sermon on the Mount, from which this statement arises, Jesus sometimes quotes from the Torah, but not always. He did not say he was quoting from the Torah at that point.

I want to close by apologising if I have put you on the defensive by any of my questions. But I am counting on you to do the same with me. I am learning from you and I want to learn more. I feel so honoured in having this privilege to dialogue with an erudite rabbi and an Israeli of your stature. If more of this sort of thing could take place, there would be an ever-increasing mutual understanding and respect between Jews and Christians – not to mention more love than ever.

Finally, if all Israeli Jews were like you, despite what the Fundamentalists may wish for, hostilities would surely diminish in our beloved Holy Land – so precious to both of us – and it would be a safer place.

Yours
RT

Letter 5

Dear RT

Please do not apologise for your straight talk – especially when it is done respectfully and graciously as you do so. Moreover, I do not feel put on the defensive and am happy to answer your questions and challenges, to the best of my ability.

However, you raise so much in your brief epistle that it's difficult to know where to start or finish. In fact I'm sure that some points will have to wait for later discussion.

Let me first of all address those subjects that we have already discussed and where I need to clarify my positions to you.

You are puzzled by my comments concerning belief. Part of the problem is our failure to clarify our definitions of terms. What do we mean by 'belief'? Is it the same as 'faith' or 'trust'? In the Hebrew language (and the 'Hebrew biblical mind' – if I may use such a term!) they are indeed much the same thing. The words imply a sense of confidence, usually with good reason (i.e. experience). But this is not the same thing as a 'command' to believe or a 'duty' to believe. The 'ancient Hebrew mind' would not have comprehended such a concept. God is the ultimate reality. His presence was a given – obvious, understood and affirmed. Moreover, if for some reason a person was blind to the obvious, telling him that he *has* to see would be meaningless! If any of the biblical phrases you have quoted cannot be understood in this light, please demand further clarification from me.

If I understand Christian faith correctly (obviously as an outside observer), belief is a very different thing from just having trust and confidence. It is of a transcendent quality that relates to the salvation of one's soul. Judaism does not teach such an idea. It *does* teach that God wants us to follow a way of life of holy and moral observance. Those who follow that way of life are indeed those to whom I refer as 'observant' and 'religious' (although I recognise that there are many spiritual Jews who may be called religious in that sense who are not very observant; however, for Orthodox Jews, religiosity and observance are very much intertwined). Theoretically it is possible (albeit unlikely) for a Jew to doubt the existence of God and still observe the religious way of life of Judaism. Why would he want to? Perhaps because the way of life is the essence of his identity; or perhaps because he experiences it as so 'good' that he appreciates its value. Of course, if one does perceive God's presence all around and within one, and one believes that the Jewish way of life is divinely revealed, one is likely to have a far more intense commitment to it, but the value of the pudding is precisely in the eating (if I may be so crass!).

You ask if there is a penalty for unbelief. Our sages of the Mishnah declare that 'the reward of the good deed is the good deed itself; and the punishment for transgression is in the transgression itself'. In other words, if you love your neighbour as yourself, no one is the richer for it than you. If you steal from him, you have done yourself far more harm than the one you have stolen from. Moreover, as far as unbelief is concerned, it is questionable as to whether this can be described as a transgression. I would call it a 'mental block' – perhaps the result of secular conditioning. I might and do regret the fact, but I cannot imagine that God would want someone to be punished for an incapacity!

But let's leave the agnostic aside for a moment and consider the believer who is a sinner – a more offensive person to my mind (e.g. someone who claims to be religious but swindles or even just takes advantage of people's ignorance to pursue material gains). Even this sinner remains a Jew by virtue of being part of the People of the Covenant. He is a bad Jew – but still a Jew. And none of us can declare him otherwise, as much as we may wish to! Such a transgressor should be punished, and indeed would be punished in a theocratic context (though according to Jewish jurisprudence such a context has to reflect the volition of the majority).

In modern democratic societies it is difficult for voluntary associations to initiate sanctions against their members (and one may even question the desirability and effectiveness of such). However, in the past and in certain cases and places even today, social sanctions and even restrictions regarding participation in religious ceremonies have been employed against those guilty of serious offences.

You are correct, RT, in your summary of the distinction between us regarding sin and sinning. Moreover, our traditional understanding of the verse in Psalm 51 to which you refer is not that the sexual act is sinful, nor that the child inherits sin.

In keeping with Genesis, we see the human person as inherently good, and in keeping with Deuteronomy (24:16) affirm the principle of personal responsibility as opposed to vicarious guilt. However, our understanding of the phraseology that the psalmist uses in Psalm 51 is of a graphic portrayal of how this capacity to err is there (indeed, by virtue of free will) at the beginning of the creation of the human being. The traditional Jewish view of Adam and Eve's sin is that, while there were consequences of their actions, it did not change the inherent human condition of being essentially good. Thus we reject the concept of 'original sin'.

Of course, this is not unrelated to the 'Messiah' question. You know that the Hebrew term 'Messiah' means one who is anointed for a particular task. In its biblical use in reference to a king or to the high priest, for example, it always relates to a (fallible) human being who has been appointed for a particular service or task. The Jewish expectation of the Messianic Age resulted from the condition of exile and thus expressed the anticipation of return to the land of Israel and a renewal of the rule of the Davidic royal household. Accordingly, the scion of that household who would be a wise leader at that time is referred to as the Messiah. However, even as far as the political redemption of the Jewish people from exile and oppression is concerned, it is God who is the Redeemer, not the Messiah.

The Messiah therefore has a functional role for society. From a Jewish perspective, the condition of one's personal soul has nothing to do with the identity of the Messiah, but is a matter between the individual and God. So here we see another big difference between us and another example of where we share sources and terms which, however, we understand very differently (and as a result often have unrealistic expectations of each other and disappointments accordingly.)

In fact, the identity of the Messiah is quite peripheral to the essence of my faith as a Jew, which is my understanding of how God wants me to live my life here and now. For me, not only does the identity of the Messiah have nothing to do with the state of my soul, it has nothing to do with the divine character. But for the Christian, if I am not mistaken, it does have to do with both of these, as the identity of the Messiah is inextricably bound up with the Divinity itself and is at the heart of your religious affirmation. Thus your 'second chance' that you hold out for me seems to be predicated upon an erroneous assumption.

I often echo the words of the late brilliant Orthodox Jewish scholar David Flusser, who declared that when the Messiah arrives (tomorrow, as we pray!) he will approach him with his Christian friends and say, 'Excuse me, Sir, have you been here before?' And if he responds affirmatively it will be clear that Christians were right all along! But the truth is that this cute comment avoids the full issue. The real issue is not just whether Jesus of Nazareth is the Messiah, but what that function means!

When the majority of Jews originally denied his messianic claim, they simply stated what they saw and understood as a result. The Messianic Age as envisaged by the prophets of Israel would mean an end of foreign oppression, the ingathering of the exiles and an era of universal peace. They saw none of these, thus they did not see any reason to acknowledge that any Messiah had arrived.

If I understand correctly, the first Christians had a religious experience that convinced them not only that Jesus was indeed the messianic figure, but that the rest of the Jews did not really understand the deeper, truer meaning of the messianic role. As I understand it, not only did Christianity claim that the social and political expectations would be fulfilled in a Second Coming (which as far as the majority of the Jews were concerned was a completely new idea, as the prophets present the messianic advent as one fully successful era), but it also claimed that, in effect, if one believed in Jesus as the Messiah then one was indeed no longer in exile and was in a state of true peace! Now to understand the messianic idea that way, you have to have that conviction – that faith! We who are not Christians do not have it. What good will it do me – from your perspective – if I were to acknowledge Jesus as the Messiah, when all it means to me is that he is a wise leader at a time of universal conflict resolution and political harmony?!

Because the Jewish messianic expectation is a political as well as a social and moral one, there were and are many Jews who saw and see the establishment of the state of Israel as 'the first flowering of our redemption', i.e. the beginning of a messianic process. These people are often described as Religious Zionists, and I would say that this is the outlook of the majority of modern Orthodox Jews and I would include myself among them. Zionism was, however, bitterly opposed by the ultra-Orthodox Jews (often incorrectly labelled 'Hassidic' – we'll leave that one for another discussion!). Ultra-Orthodoxy (referred to in Hebrew as *haredi*) was and is a reactionary withdrawal from secular society (as opposed to modern Orthodoxy, which seeks to find a balance between being a religious observant Jew on the one hand and living in the modern world and being a part of a wider culture on the other). Because Zionism was led by people who were not religiously observant (and often even hostile towards Jewish traditionalism), the ultra-Orthodox saw it as just a Jewish form of the devil they wanted to have nothing to do with – namely, the secular world. Moreover, the idea that this return and establishment of Jewish sovereignty had any religious significance, let alone messianic relevance, they saw/see as an impiety, if not a heresy. Most of them believe that the whole messianic fulfilment will come miraculously, and only be manifest in a fully religiously observant society. Eventually, after the Shoah (the Holocaust) and the establishment of the State of Israel, they came to pragmatic terms with Zionism, but they still did and do not see the political movement of establishing Jewish sovereignty in the land as having any religious, let alone messianic, significance.

I was both brought up in and (as I indicated) consider myself to be part of the Religious Zionist camp. However, I believe that there are those (far too many) who have allowed this perception of the prophetic (messianic) significance of Israel to go to their head and warp their good sense and even their moral values. I refer to many of the religious Zionist settlers in the West Bank and their supporters, who are so eschatologically convinced of the messianic significance of Israel that they ignore the political, economic, demographic and moral consequences of their actions and ideology. I believe that not only is this very dangerous (and actually threatens Israel's very survival) but it is in complete conflict with biblical/ Jewish teaching and in fact makes an important means – the land of Israel – into an end in itself. That, RT, is to my mind idolatry – no less! To transgress our moral values and teaching in order to preserve a Jewish polity is to me a contradiction in terms.

As I mentioned in my last letter, our relationship to the land of Israel is conditional on our behaviour. As I say, I do believe Zionism to have messianic significance, but that doesn't mean that its success is guaranteed. It can still fail, God forbid, and unless we behave wisely as well as morally, it will do so. As I also mentioned to you, this means that we are duty bound to seek a territorial compromise with those who are not Jews who also live in the land, both because we do have biblically mandated moral obligations towards all human beings – all created in the Divine Image – and also out of enlightened necessity. If we try to hold on to it all right now, we may, God forbid, lose it all again.

So how far am I prepared to go, you ask. As far as I am concerned, as far as we have to! I hope that we will not have to give up the Old City of Jerusalem, and I believe that we can still arrive at a political resolution that could enable Jerusalem to be part and parcel of both Israel and a Palestinian state at the same time. If, however, there is no alternative, then just as Israel managed to develop Jewish life in an independent state without the Old City of Jerusalem until 1967 we should be prepared to do so again, if this is the price of peace and guaranteeing our future.

If this tragic necessity actually happens, it will not stop my praying and longing once more for the day when we can live again in all of Jerusalem, in the same way as I continue to pray – like all Orthodox Jews – for the eventual reconstruction of the Temple and the restoration of its service. In practice, however, the latter is not a simple matter. You may have seen, RT, the signs at the entrances to the Temple Mount set up by the Chief Rabbinate of Israel (sic!) telling Jews not to enter the precinct of the Temple Mount! This is precisely because Judaism teaches that the area where the Temple stood is intrinsically holy (in fact, the only place on this earth that is totally intrinsically holy!) and, as when the Temple stood, so today we may not tread upon the ground there in a state of ritual impurity. The Bible in Leviticus lays down the rites of ritual purification that require elements which we no longer have (most specifically the ashes of the pure red heifer). Moreover, we are not exactly sure where the precise boundaries of the Temple and the Holy of Holies are; and as this knowledge is essential for any legitimate reconstruction, all these factors make it practically impossible for us today to rebuild the Temple – even if the whole Muslim as well as Christian world were to beg us to do so!

As a result, the mainstream Jewish tradition over the last millennium has been that the Third Temple would appear supernaturally in a pillar of fire from Heaven.

Even after 1967 when Israel acquired control of the Old City of Jerusalem, the Temple Mount has remained in Muslim hands, and Israel passed a law that year guaranteeing the integrity and maintenance of the holy sites for their respective religions. This has not only been out of Israel's political good sense, but also precisely because of the aforementioned mainstream Orthodox Jewish teaching. I see the traditional restrictions in Judaism against going on to the Temple Mount as a blessing in the present context of conflict between Palestinians and Israelis, and as providing the means for ensuring that no tradition should feel that its holy sites are threatened by the attachments of another tradition. Naturally, this is until the Almighty deems the full messianic advent to have arrived. And then it will be in an era of universal peace anyway, so whatever happens there and then will have happened peacefully and by agreement!

As I say, all Orthodox Jews pray for that day when the Temple will be rebuilt and its service reintroduced. However, you may recall, RT, that my family and I are vegetarians, and like Rabbi Abraham Isaac Kuk, the first Ashkenazi Chief Rabbi in the Holy Land, I believe that when that Temple service is restored, it will be vegetarian in practice and will no longer require animal offerings. But perhaps we should leave the subject of vegetarianism for a future exchange, as I think that I've already touched on quite a lot for the time being. As I expected, I have not managed to answer all your questions in this letter, so please press me on those you want to make sure that I do not avoid.

Yours
David

Letter 6

Dear David

It was such a pleasure to be with you in Jerusalem since our last correspondence. Louise, our son TR and I enjoyed our Shabbat meal with you so very much. As the first time we met was over a Shabbat meal, I was so thrilled that my family could now have a taste of this. I could only wish that there were many Christian families that do the equivalent at least once a week. What an example you set for us, David and Sharon.

Before I respond to your last letter I wanted to answer a question you put to me just as we began to partake of the Shabbat meal. You will recall that you introduced the meal by sanctifying the day with the blessing over the wine, celebrating God's creation. Then, after the ritual washing of the hands, you broke one of the two loaves of bread. You indicated that these represent the double portion of manna that came down on the eve of Sabbaths and festivals for the children of Israel during their wandering in the desert to keep them from working by collecting the manna on the holy days. You then gave thanks for divine providence and asked me a question I have given serious thought to since (which I will paraphrase): did Jesus intend that the Lord's Supper should be continued by his disciples *in addition* to the Sabbath and festival rituals with their own original meaning, or did he want the Lord's Supper to *replace* such rituals?

Very good question. My answer is, Jesus intended that the Lord's Supper should replace the ancient rituals because he became our Passover Lamb. The Last Supper was not a Shabbat meal (although there may have been similarities) but Passover. When Jesus said, 'This bread is my body and this wine is my blood,' he was announcing that he himself – God's lamb without spot or blemish – fulfilled Passover. There would therefore be no need to keep up the observance of Passover, which was not only carried out in gratitude to God for the miraculous deliverance from Pharaoh but also *pointed to* its perfect fulfilment in Jesus dying on the Cross for our sins. The sprinkled blood over the door and on each side at Passover would anticipate the day when blood flowed from Jesus' head and hands. We therefore keep Passover when we eat the bread and wine at the Lord's Supper in remembrance of him.

However, it is not uncommon for messianic believers (Jews who have accepted Jesus Christ as Messiah and Lord) to practise many of the ancient rituals because this reminds them of their original meaning and fulfilment. I see this as a good thing for them to do. It seems to me that this is not only a way of teaching essential doctrine but, just maybe, it could be a testimony – even an evangelistic opportunity – for Jews generally to learn more about their theological roots, not to mention to Jews who already take the Old Testament seriously. Therefore, although Jesus intended that the Lord's Supper would replace the ancient Jewish rituals, there is no harm in observing them when one knows it is not a requirement.

When it comes to the Law – ceremonial (the way God's ancient people should worship), civil (how they should govern themselves), moral (the Ten Commandments) – and the way that Law is interpreted in the New Testament, the key word for us is 'fulfilment'. If in purchasing real estate nowadays the issue – as they say – is 'location, location, location', I would say that the relationship to the Law and the gospel, the Old Testament and the New Testament, is 'fulfilment, fulfilment, fulfilment'. This will almost certainly be a recurring theme in our correspondence so I will now address issues your last letter raised.

A profound distinction between us, as you say, is the matter of faith, or belief. You contend that there is no command 'to believe' in ancient Israel. Since you are obviously the expert on the nature of the ancient Hebrew mind I will ask you please to forgive me if I don't grasp what you mean. My opinion would be based not on what I know about the Hebraic mind but upon Old Testament Scripture. For example, was it not *faith* that lay behind the ancient Israelites' keeping the Passover? They must have believed that God spoke to them through Moses. It was surely based entirely on *command*. They would not have obeyed this unprecedented command if they did not believe it. So their faith must have been preceded by a command to believe. 'The Israelites did just what the LORD commanded Moses and Aaron' (Exod. 12:28). You also stated that Judaism does not teach the idea that faith relates to the salvation of one's soul. But would not any Jew have been destroyed the night of Passover had they not honoured Moses' command? It seems to me this indicates that there is a connection between faith and the salvation of one's soul.

I would therefore want to argue that not only would the Israelites not have kept the command had they not first of all believed, but that God even prepared them for faith. You will recall that Moses' initial anxiety about his own calling was precisely how he himself would be accepted, or believed, by the Israelites. This is why he asked the Lord, 'What shall I tell them?' when they ask why they should believe Moses. God then said to him, 'I AM WHO I AM. This is what you are to say to the Israelites: "I AM has sent me to you"' (Exod. 3:13–14). The Israelites understandably needed some convincing, but when they were eventually persuaded, it is written that 'they *believed* ... they bowed down and worshipped' (Exod. 4:31).

Not only that; later on, when Joshua and Caleb were opposed by the Israelites (who were afraid to press on and enter the Promised Land), God was angry with Israel. This was because they did not believe that God would be with them to overcome the inhabitants of Canaan. 'We seemed like grasshoppers in our own eyes, and we looked the same to them' (Num. 13:33). God swore in his wrath, of that generation, 'They shall never enter my rest' (Ps. 95:11). There was surely but one reason for this: they did not enter in because of their unbelief. Only Caleb and Joshua entered the Promised Land later on, the rest having died in the wilderness – as God swore would happen. This, to me, shows an important difference between the state of the souls of those who died in the desert and the souls of Joshua and Caleb. This historic incident in ancient Israelite history, I would have thought, shows an essential connection between faith and the state of one's soul.

This issue is made equally clear by the premise of Habakkuk's prophecy which was based on living by the faithfulness of God. The quotation of Habakkuk 2:4, 'The righteous shall live by his faithfulness' (quoted three times from the LXX [Septuagint] in the New Testament as 'the just shall live by faith' – Rom. 1:17, Gal. 3:11, Heb. 10:38), was couched in the promise that God would reveal himself eventually but unmistakably. 'For the revelation awaits an appointed time; it speaks of the end and will not prove false. Though it linger, wait for it; it will certainly come and will not delay' (Hab. 2:3). Then came that significant word, as you, David, know in Hebrew, which says, 'The righteous shall live by his [God's] faithfulness' (v. 4). Living by the faithfulness of God is *faith*, and this became the foundation for the New Testament teaching of justification by faith. It was based entirely upon the Old Testament promises and the fulfilment of them through (1) the person and death of Jesus and (2) one's transferring their trust in good works to what Jesus accomplished for us.

I want to say therefore that faith, or the command to believe, as we Christians believe, is nothing new. It is not a New Testament innovation but the heart of Israel's reason for existence. They *believed* they were chosen; they *believed* they had a future; and it was entirely because they believed God's Word to them through the Law and the prophets. It was surely the basis and impetus for living in every servant of God in ancient Israel. It is what motivated the great men and women of the Old Testament to do what they did; the absence of it incurred the wrath of Yahweh again and again.

I was therefore surprised to hear you say that there is no warning in Judaism against not recognising the Messiah. Did I grasp what you were saying? 'The identity of the Messiah is quite peripheral to the essence of my faith as a Jew,' you say. You preceded this by saying 'the condition of one's personal soul has nothing to do with the identity of the Messiah'. Does this mean that God is saying that Israel can 'take it or leave it' (as to the acceptance of Messiah) and all is still well in their relationship with him? It is good if they recognise him, but 'not to worry' if they don't? Unless I have misinterpreted you (please correct me, this is important), it is no wonder that Jews would not be disturbed – then or now – whether or not Messiah came and they missed him! They remain Jews either way and that is apparently the important thing.

Am I right to think, then, that the crux of the disagreement between us thus comes to this: any Jew is a saved Jew – even if he or she does not believe? It comes down to ethnicity, race or culture, but not faith. Is there no further responsibility for a Jew insofar as the state of one's soul is concerned? And if there is life beyond the grave, the only qualification for bliss in the resurrection is that one was a Jew? Please do tell me, David, if I have got this wrong, because it would not be very productive if we continue to correspond under such a major misunderstanding.

I need to ask you another question. I realise you do not want to be associated with the attitude and self-righteousness of those Pharisees the New Testament describes. But would you have in common with them the teaching of the resurrection of the dead and life beyond the grave? To put it another way, was Jesus being faithful to Pharisaical teaching, or was it his own contribution, when he said, 'A time is coming when all who are in their graves will hear his voice and come out – those who have done well will rise to live, and those who have done evil will rise to be condemned' (John 5:28–9)? This teaching was, as I understand it, an essential difference between Pharisees and Sadducees; the latter did not believe in life beyond the grave or in the resurrection of the body. But Pharisees did. So I am assuming you do, too. Therefore, what determines the status of one's soul after death? Is it only being a Jew – whether one be a Pharisee, Sadducee or atheist?

As for unbelief being a 'mental block', I think I know what you mean by that. For that is precisely what has set in on Jews (speaking generally), according to Paul in Romans 11. Your view is that God would not be fair in judging a person because of their incapacity, by which I think you mean an incapacity, or inability, to believe. I understand what you mean. But on the other hand, is this not God's prerogative? He said to Moses, 'I will have mercy on whom I will have mercy, and I will have compassion on whom I will have compassion' (Exod. 33:19). He also said that his ways are higher than our ways and his thoughts are higher than our thoughts (Isa. 55:8–9).

I would therefore argue, David, that God does sometimes command us to do what *seems* unfair or unreasonable. He commanded Abraham to sacrifice Isaac (Gen. 22:2). He commanded Moses to 'raise your staff and stretch out your hand over the sea to divide the water' when the people were trapped with the Egyptians behind them (Exod. 14:15). Had Moses kept crying out to God that he had a mental block, God would not have been pleased. But Moses did what he was required to do. It required faith. And God wonderfully acted. According to Jesus and Paul, the Jews rejected the One offered to them and, as a consequence, were inflicted with a 'spirit of stupor, eyes so that they could not see and ears so that they could not hear' (Rom. 11:8, echoing Deut. 29:4 and Isa. 29:10). And yet, like it or not, all of us (whether Jew or Gentile) are equally commanded to believe. Those who turn to the Lord Jesus are given faith in that moment.

I therefore have in mind continually when I write to you, David, that it is such a great privilege to speak to you like this. You are an exceedingly rare person to engage in this kind of candour. I know too that there is no amount of persuasion that I can muster, however airtight my logic or irrefutable my biblical interpretation, that can convince you. 'A man convinced against his will is of the same opinion still.' It is only by the grace of the Holy Spirit that your eyes, or anybody else's, will be opened. It is by the sheer grace of God that my own eyes were opened. But at the same time I have a responsibility to speak to you with all the love and persuasion I have. I want you to see what is clear to me. If I cross over a line when I have misunderstood or misinterpreted you, or you feel I am pressing you too far, I thank you with all my heart for telling me. But you have known from the outset that I have a desire for you to know Jesus not according to the flesh but as revealed by the Holy Spirit.

You will smile when I tell you that, at first, I honestly wondered if you were a secret believer in Jesus! Your gracious and magnanimous spirit made me think you must be a

Christian! I'm serious! I know too many Christians who should learn from your attitude and kindness. But as we continued with our correspondence I was forced to admit that you are not a believer in Jesus – quite the contrary. But your openness and courage bless me no end none the less.

Speaking of courage, I am amazed at your position with regard to Jerusalem and the Temple Mount. I never dreamed I would hear an Orthodox Jewish rabbi be willing to concede the ancient city of Jerusalem, including the Temple Mount, if that is what would guarantee Israel's safety and existence. You say you hope that you do not have to give up the Old City, but you would do it (as was done before) 'if this is the price of peace and guaranteeing our future'. This to me shows an awful lot of honesty and courage. You must have come under a lot of criticism from your fellow Orthodox Jews, not to mention rabbis. I think you would also be criticised by a lot of Christians, especially in America, who think that the Temple Mount must be occupied (and the Temple rebuilt) by Jews before Jesus can come back! So if the concession of the Old City were to be adopted by the Israeli government, the Second Coming would be postponed for a long time – except for one thing: the Bible nowhere indicates that the Temple must be rebuilt before the Second Coming.

By the way, it is this same type of Christian – not me – who teaches that Jews are to be given a 'second chance'. This is certainly not my own position. If it were left up to me, yes, David, I would want to give you and your family and all Jews – and everybody in the world who ever lived – a second chance (even though you hint that it is not of any great concern to you). I raise this only because you wrote in your last letter, 'Thus your "second chance" that you hold out for me seems to be predicated upon an erroneous assumption.' I am sorry I have not made my position clear. The 'second chance' some Christians offer Jews is without any warrant whatever in

Scripture. This notion is taking the *specialness* of Jews too far; it is predicated upon a severe misunderstanding of God's special place for Israel. It is absolutely true that God's ancient people are special. I agree that *you* are special. No doubt about that. I envy you. But neither you nor I are in the position of being granted a 'second chance' when Jesus comes again. There is not a hint of this in the Bible. So I would not want you to think I am with those who treat you in this fashion. Although such people love Jews – as I do – we would do you no favour to perpetuate this, if we really do love you. It is a risk of incalculable proportion to teach anything which could lead a Jew (or anyone else) to say, 'Oh well, if I do not accept Jesus as my Messiah, I will get a second chance anyway.' I wish it were true!

What you seem to be saying in that part of your last letter is this. The Messiah you envisage (whom you are still looking for) is not divine in the first place. The Messiah that Israel awaits, if I interpret you correctly, never was envisaged to be God in the flesh who would die on a cross and be raised from the dead, but rather a charismatic political and military leader who would restore the glory to ancient Israel, rebuild the Temple and become to his people much like what King David had been. In any case, you are talking about a man, very human – certainly not Deity. If I understand you, this is why a 'second chance' does not matter to you. It is because the Messiah you will recognise would not punish you if you did not recognise him. This is the reason, I believe you are saying, the salvation of one's soul is not connected to the identity of the Messiah.

Before I close this letter, let me summarise generally what I perceive to be three major differences between us so far. First, the matter of faith. Second, the nature of the Messiah. Would I be right to think that you believe the Messiah we Christians accept – Jesus – never saw himself as God, that the Church in the following century created this understanding of him? I note in your first letter that the late date of Matthew is important to you. But apart from dates, whether viewing the synoptic Gospels, the Gospel of John or the writings of Paul, it is essential to our belief that the One who came was the one Isaiah saw hundreds of years in advance, who would be called 'Wonderful Counsellor, Mighty God, Everlasting Father, Prince of Peace' (Isa. 9:6). And that his death meant that the Lord laid on him our iniquity (Isa. 53:6). This brings me to the third big difference between us: namely, the nature of sin. I will postpone further comments on this until I hear from you next. But if I have not given adequate attention to any matter you have raised, please tell me.

Yours
RT

Letter 7

Dear RT

While there are things you write as a profession of your faith on which I would not presume to comment, let alone argue, I am truly grateful that you probe and challenge me the way you do – above all because it enables me to clarify my own positions to you and anyone who reads our exchange, to the best of my ability.

It is clear from your latest response that I did not do so very well in my last letter and I need to restate certain comments more clearly.

Of course faith is very important in Judaism! What I had indicated, however, is that to live God's revealed way of life (the commandments) as manifest to us in the Torah (the Pentateuch and the Oral Tradition) is the *most* important thing for Judaism. As I said, it is difficult to imagine why someone would want to commit him or herself to living this way of life without faith in God, but it is theoretically possible. In other words, what I am saying that Judaism precisely rejects, as being of little or no value, is a faith that does not lead to action. So you have indeed 'got me wrong'!

I will discuss the word 'saved' below. But let me initially use it as if we have a shared lexicon here. No, a Jew is not 'saved' individually because of her or his ethnicity. A Jew is 'saved' because he or she leads a way of life in keeping with God's commandments. In fact, in a way it is harder for a Jew to be 'saved' because she or he is expected to observe more commandments. Judaism teaches that prior to the Covenant with Abraham, Isaac and Jacob and their descendants, God established a Covenant with all humanity (reflecting divine love for all) with the children of Noah after the Flood. Covenant is a two-way process; and rabbinic understanding of human responsibilities in this regard is that all people should observe the prohibitions against idolatry, murder, sexual misconduct, blasphemy, stealing, eating part of an animal alive, and the positive obligation to establish courts of justice and abide by them. Every Gentile who follows such a way of life, according to Rabbinic Judaism, is guaranteed his or her 'portion in the world to come'. That is all Judaism understands in the term 'saved'. As I have noted, we do not see humans as originally evil or condemned, but in fact as being intrinsically good. Sin is the inevitable consequence of freedom of choice and it is that which deforms (or 'condemns') our souls. Sincere repentance is what redeems our souls from the consequence of sin, and in that sense our souls may said to be 'saved' by repentance (as I have mentioned, the Hebrew word teshuvah literally means a process of 'returning' – returning to God and our naturally good proximate relationship to Him and His way).

Rabbinic Judaism, as the heir of Pharisaic Judaism, believes emphatically in the concept of the afterlife or continuity of the soul and the reward (i.e. the consequence of our good actions) that the soul enjoys accordingly. However, precisely as this is the direct result of how we have lived our lives in this world, the Jewish emphasis is upon the latter, albeit in the full knowledge that 'this world is like a vestibule before the banqueting hall'.

The Sinai Covenant with the children of Israel revealed a far more demanding way of life than the Noahide Covenant. By living this way of life, the children of Israel would both enjoy its spiritual benefits and also testify to the Divine Presence in their midst. However, taking on these responsibilities means in effect that it is actually more demanding for the Jew than the Gentile to guarantee his/her portion in the world to come. Judaism teaches that righteous Gentiles, as righteous Jews, have their portion (reward) in the world to come. Moreover, in keeping with Judaic teaching regarding infinite divine compassion, great Jewish thinkers like Maimonides have believed that it takes an inordinately evil individual to destroy any goodness in his or her divine soul and thus of any reward/continuity. I should mention here as a footnote that there have been various Jewish interpretations of concepts that in English we call Heaven, Hell and Purgatory, but all interpretations see them as the consequences of our behaviour, not of declarations or manifestos.

Of course, more often than not there is – and indeed there should be – an inextricable link between what we declare and what we do. But you know, RT, as well as I, that this is not always necessarily the case. Above all, what I'm saying in this regard is that Judaism does not consider a declaration of faith or even a sincere belief to have any redeeming value in itself.

As I mentioned in my previous letter, the Hebrew word 'faith' is generally synonymous with 'trust' and relates to experience. Thus when after the crossing of the Red Sea it says 'and the children of Israel believed in God and Moses his servant', it clearly indicates that their *experience* had convinced them of God's omnipresence and omnipotence as well as of Moses' divinely mandated leadership.

Yes indeed, as I tried to clarify in my previous letter, most practising Jews today, like the children of Israel then, observe the commandments out of conviction that their source is the God in whom they believe. Until modern times the very idea of non-belief would have been an unthinkable idea. However, my point again is that belief in itself is of little or no value unless it leads to action. This is normative Jewish teaching and it is indeed one of the fundamental points of variance with Christian teaching, which if I am not mistaken sees faith in itself as being of redeeming value.

I trust you can now see all the biblical texts that you quote in this light as well. We interpret them according to our own religious world view – e.g. the reason that the children of Israel who did not hearken to Joshua and Caleb did not enter the land was that they *demonstrated* their lack of commitment to God's promise. That indeed reflected an inadequate faith in God Himself. But even if they would not have had full faith in God Himself but would have still followed His charge, they would have then entered and possessed the land!

Incidentally, our translation of Habakkuk 2:4 is 'the righteous shall live by *his [own]* Faith' (not by God's!) and we understand that to mean precisely that the righteous is only the one who actually lives, in practice, the implications of his or her faith.

Probably part of the reason for your misunderstanding of what I wrote is my failure to emphasise the difference between the individual (Jew's) relationship with God, and the collective relationship of the children of Israel with God. As far as the latter is concerned, Judaism teaches that a Jew is always part of a covenanted collective whose eternity is assured by God and for whom divine forgiveness and restoration are guaranteed. However, the individual is totally personally responsible for his or her actions; and depending upon how one has led one's life, the individual Jew merits to 'enter the Garden of Eden' (Heaven) or does not (Gehinnom or Hell).

Similarly, Orthodox Judaism teaches the principle of the resurrection of the dead, and it is one of Maimonides' Thirteen Principles of Faith that has come to be accepted as a virtual theological credo by Orthodox Jews (and appears in the daily prayer book as such). However, Maimonides elsewhere (as I have indicated) dwells extensively on the concept of the afterlife (the continuity of the soul) but doesn't mention this in the Thirteen Principles. Accordingly, many commentators have assumed that, for him, the two are one and the same, and resurrection refers to the spiritual ascent of the soul after the body dies. Others have precisely interpreted the concept (in keeping with Ezekiel chapter 36) to refer to the collective resurrection of the people. Certain religious Zionist thinkers have interpreted this passage of Ezekiel as anticipating the national resurrection of the Jewish people in the land of Israel when it appeared that they were just a valley of dead dry bones after the Holocaust. However, most Orthodox Jews still believe in a physical resurrection at the end of times, and in all these respects Jesus was affirming traditional Pharisaic teaching.

You have indeed correctly summarised my view (to be more precise, Jewish teaching) regarding the concept of the Messiah and its relation to the above.

Let me reiterate that the overwhelming majority of Jews did not accept Jesus as the Messiah because the prophetic idea of the Messianic Age indicated an end to foreign oppression and exile and this did not happen. However, your suggestion that they didn't care about it one way or another because they would remain Jews is misleading, precisely because the one does not have anything to do with the other. The Jews then were *eagerly* awaiting a Messiah who would deliver them from Roman subjugation to be free to lead their religious and national life. It is quite possible (even probable) that Jesus did think that God was going to deliver them from that oppression at that time, and perhaps he did expect to be the one who would be the wise leader of the nation – the Messiah. However, you are correct in assuming that I personally do not think for one minute that Jesus saw himself in terms of the theological construct that Christianity affirms.

Finally, I wish to pursue your kind answer to my question about whether or not Jesus wanted his disciples to continue to observe the commandments and rituals revealed in or based on the Hebrew Bible. Your answer, in essence, is no; as the New Testament has fulfilled the Old Testament, there is no need to do so, although you don't see anything wrong with it if there are those who wish to introduce such observances into their lives today (even though they are unnecessary).

You even suggest that moral teachings are also fulfilled through faith in Jesus. Does this mean that one can be immoral and still be 'saved' – in Christian terms? If you distinguish between moral and ritual teachings in the Hebrew Bible, on what basis do you do so? For example, the Fourth Commandment in the Decalogue dealing with the Sabbath is surely replete with moral purpose and content. I am very puzzled by this and look forward to your further clarification.

I might add in relation to this question and my earlier comments that as a believing and practising Jew, I understand ritual commandments as well as moral commandments to have a religious ethical purpose. As our ancient sages declare, 'the commandments were given in order to ennoble people'. The term the Hebrew Bible uses to describe, for example, the purpose of the dietary laws (Deut. 14:2, 21) or of the Sabbath observance (Exod. 20:8) is 'holiness'. In fact, 'holiness' is stated in the Bible as the purpose of all the commandments (Num. 15:40). In modern parlance, one might call holiness 'God consciousness' (more of an 'awareness' of reality than a supra-rational 'faith').

A fully believing observant Jew is conscious of the Divine

Presence not only when praying three times a day, not only when encountering his/her neighbour – each and every one created in the Divine Image – but also when he or she eats and drinks, works and rests and in many other daily and weekly activities.

Our sages declare (in the concluding Midrash, or rabbinic homily, on the Pentateuch) that if one rises in the morning and does not bless God for the sunrise, or retires at night without having blessed God for sunset, one is 'like a dead person'. To understand this cryptic comment one needs to know that in Jewish practice one makes a blessing before partaking of any pleasure, food or drink. Thus before eating an apple, for example, an observant Jew recites a formula as follows: 'Blessed are You, O Lord our God, Sovereign of the Universe, who creates fruit of the trees.' In so doing, one is raising a basic activity – eating – to a higher level of consciousness. One does not just instinctively bite into the apple but pauses to acknowledge Divine Providence and to give thanks for the sustenance and pleasure one is about to enjoy. Therefore, our sages are saying in that Midrash that if one's life is without awareness of the Divine Presence in the beauty of the creation around one, and indeed in one's neighbour and oneself, then one is not really living. One's body might be functioning, but one's soul is not really alive!

Accordingly, for the believing observant Jew the commandments are not only no chore, but a source of joy and beauty ennobling our lives; and even when Jews have experienced darkness outside around them (unfortunately more often than not in the course of history) they have known the light and beauty of the observance of the Torah that has sustained us throughout the ages. As King David declares, 'If it were not for the delight of Your Torah, I would have perished in my affliction' (Ps. 119:92). For faithful observant Jews, in the very observance of the commandments not only do we find life, beauty and joy, but we also find divine testimony, love and salvation.

Yours
David

Letter 8

Dear David

It is interesting to me that the more we write to each other, the more I understand the nature of the particular issues we are discussing. The issues appear much the same as I outlined in my previous letter: (1) the nature of faith; (2) the nature of the Messiah; and (3) the nature of sin. The nature of faith has broadened to include the way of salvation; the nature of the Messiah now touches on the messianic consciousness of Jesus; the matter of sin comes down to whether a person is a sinner *before* he or she sins or if actual sinning is the *only* thing that makes one a sinner.

I suppose I should not be surprised that we would be on opposite sides of some of these issues so soon, and yet it is illuminating to me none the less that these matters have surfaced almost naturally. All this has arisen because of the original question that led to our correspondence in the first place: 'What is a Pharisee?' Perhaps more issues will emerge, but your latest instalment confirms these three things all the more. I don't think I was prepared for how much I would learn from our exchanges, so I am exceedingly grateful to you for helping to clarify these things by the gracious and articulate way you have written.

You began your last instalment by saying there are things regarding my profession of faith you would not presume to comment on, 'let alone argue'. But surely, David, you must! You will recall that when the idea for our correspondence was conceived at the Mount Zion Hotel in Jerusalem, it was agreed that you would show why you should *remain* an Orthodox Jew and not be a Christian, and that I should write to show why you *should* embrace Jesus as your promised Messiah. So I hope you will comment, even argue if you like, or I will think you are being convinced by me!

And yet I hope you will comment on the aspects of my profession of faith for another reason. I know, David, that you looked carefully at the verses I quoted, so please forgive me for repeating some of them. I guess I might worry that you could easily and unwittingly gloss over what is vital to me, namely, the very reason I believe you must do what most Jews in history have not done: *honestly examine* these Scriptures and consequently accept Jesus – *Yeshua* – as your own Messiah. You may think that the fulfilment of my wish to see you look at Jesus in this way is out of the question. But I lovingly plead with you none the less to look carefully again at the very Scriptures I put to you. It should be *easy* for you – you are the natural olive tree (Rom. 11:24)! After all, moreover, you are, it seems to me, already extraordinary and unique among Orthodox Jews and rabbis. And yet I admit that, humanly speaking, what I am really after in engaging in these dialogues with you is about as feasible as trying to touch the moon!

I can almost hear you saying that you were required to look at passages like this many times – that is, to see them the way Christians interpret them – because of your training as a rabbi. I have been deeply impressed too by how much you know the New Testament. But dare I ask if you have read Old Testament passages with the view that, just maybe, they have been wrongly interpreted after all by the sages of the centuries? What about those Jews who *have* received Jesus as their promised Messiah? What made them do it?

My conversations with you are not the first attempt on my part to see a Jew receive Jesus as the promised Messiah. It has been a wish of my heart for many years. You will recall my attempts with Rabbi Abraham Kellner. But he wasn't the last. Many years ago I also had a dialogue, not in writing but in face-to-face conversations, with Nathan Darsky, a Russian Jew who came to America as a young man and became the founder of Pepsi-Cola. I used to visit him at his home in Miami Beach and he always liked it when I prayed with him. He became fond of me for some reason and would come to see Louise and me at our old home in Fort Lauderdale. On one occasion I remember praying for him virtually all day, anticipating his coming to our home that evening for a meal. I had aspirations of seeing him embrace Jesus as his Messiah. I was so sure that, upon hearing Isaiah 53, which I read to him with some commentary, he would immediately admit that the most rational explanation and obvious fulfilment of that chapter was the way the prophet foresaw how Israel would reject their promised Messiah (vv. 1–3) who came to this world with the very purpose to die on a cross (vv. 4–7).

But my friend Mr Darsky dismissed this interpretation in one stroke: 'This chapter is describing the suffering of my people the Jews.' He then elaborated on what is absolutely true, how the Jews have suffered in ancient history and recent history (he referred to the Holocaust). I might have asked him to look at Isaiah 49:6–7 – verses which are clearly promising Messiah and could not possibly refer to the suffering people of Israel. I might have pressed him to read Isaiah 52:14: 'Just as there were many who were appalled at him – his appearance was so disfigured beyond that of any man and his form marred beyond human likeness'. Or I could have read and re-read to him Isaiah 53:5–7 and 12: 'he poured out his life unto death, and was numbered with the transgressors. For he bore the sin of many, and made intercession for the transgressors', which could only be referring to a suffering individual. But I did not push him any further, I could see that all I hoped for was not about to happen. Whether anybody had put these matters to him before, or since, I do not know. Our friendship continued after that occasion. We moved away from Fort Lauderdale and he has died since. I have witnessed to Jews, including Israelis, a number of times over the years, but only one of them – a lady from Moscow (who told me later she was Jewish) – accepted Jesus as her Messiah.

All I am asking of you, David, is to *consider* certain aspects of my theology: for example, how Isaiah saw hundreds of years in advance that Israel's promised Messiah would be called the 'Mighty God, Everlasting Father' (Isa. 9:6). Is this not a promise that the coming Messiah would be *God in the flesh*? Is it not true that Isaiah also saw long before the event that the people of Israel would by and large *completely reject* their Messiah? 'Who has believed our message and to whom has the arm of the LORD been revealed?' (Isa. 53:1). Isaiah foresaw that the very One Israel had prayed for would indeed show up – but be completely underestimated and, sadly, missed entirely by most Jews. This is because, far from being charismatic and obvious, the Messiah would be like a 'root out of dry ground', a lacklustre figure without apparent attractiveness (Isa. 53:1–3). On top of that, he would be perceived by Jews as being severely but rightly judged by God (vv. 4–5) *and* he would die as a substitutionary atoning sacrifice for our sins: 'the LORD laid on him the iniquity of us all' (v. 6). I will stop at that verse for now, only to point out that the Jews who *did* believe in Jesus as their Messiah two thousand years ago – and since – have found incalculable comfort and hope from Isaiah 53.

I was relieved to hear you say that a Jew is not saved because of ethnicity. I interpret you as saying also that a Jew could lose his or her soul in Hell after death, even if that person has to be pretty awful to merit that state. But at the same time I am still amazed to think that anybody could be saved by keeping the works of the Law! If one were judged by good intentions, yes, there is hope for some of us. But if we are to be judged by whether we come up to the high standard required, namely the fulfilment of 613 pieces of Mosaic legislation, I for one would not have a chance. You say that it is harder for a Jew since he has to answer to Sinai. Are you really saying it is easier for a Gentile because he will not be judged by the Law but rather by the Covenant with Noah? I gather then you would say that I am exempt from the Law but not from the Noahide Covenant?

It is my opinion that when Jesus promised personally to fulfil the Law in Matthew 5:17, meaning not merely the Ten Commandments but – when you add them up in Exodus, Leviticus, Numbers and Deuteronomy – not only 613 but over 2,000 pieces of Mosaic legislation, it was the most stupendous statement he made: 'I have not come to abolish them [the Law or the prophets] but to fulfil them.' Nobody had done that, truly fulfilling the Mosaic Law in every jot and tittle. Nobody. Even James, who was a great defender of the Law in the earliest Church, finally agreed with Peter that even their Jewish ancestors were not able to bear the yoke of the Law (Acts 15:10–21). But when Jesus said, 'I will fulfil the Law,' it was a major statement fairly early on in his ministry. So when he uttered the words on the cross, 'It is finished' (Greek *tetelestai* – John 19:30), he was stating he had accomplished what he had promised to do – fulfil the Law – because *tetelestai* was a word also understood as 'paid in full'.

This brings us back to the nature of faith. You are right, David, in saying we regard faith in itself as being of 'redeeming value' – with one proviso: that the object of that faith is in Jesus whose substitutionary death atoned for our sins. We believe that Jesus was our *substitute*. He not only took our place by bearing the wrath of God we deserve (Matt. 27:46; 2 Cor. 5:21) but was also our substitute in having performed the righteous deeds of the Law *in our behalf* (1 Cor. 1:30). Therefore, faith justifies when I *rely* on Jesus as a person and as my Redeemer.

You asked whether a person could be immoral and still be saved. One of my predecessors at Westminster Chapel in London, Dr Martyn Lloyd-Jones, used to say that if a person having heard the gospel *does not ask that question* it probably means he hasn't yet heard the gospel! Dr Lloyd-Jones went so far as to say that if our gospel does not suggest the possibility of antinomianism (literally 'against law') we probably have not preached the gospel, but at the same time he added that if one thinks that a Christian *can* be immoral one still has not understood the gospel! The gospel inevitably engenders good works. The Christian is unequivocally called to be holy (1 Thess. 4:3). 'For we are God's workmanship, created in Christ Jesus to do good works, which God prepared in advance for us to do' (Eph. 2:10). But those works are not what saves us; it is faith alone in Yeshua alone that saves anybody. Good works flow from the *gratitude* we owe to God for giving us a Messiah who fulfilled the Law by paying our debt to it.

I mentioned James above. In his short epistle James came out so strongly for *works* that Martin Luther regarded James' letter as 'an epistle of straw'. But that was not Luther's only mistake! All Christians deeply regret statements this man made about Jews. All we can do is hang our heads in shame. As for James, he was not stating how to be saved or even how to know one is saved, but what kind of faith will make an impact on the 'poor man' (Greek *protochon* – accusative masculine singular) in James 2:6. So when James said in 2:14, 'Can faith save *him* [accusative masculine singular]?' he was still referring to the same poor man who would be singularly unimpressed with a faith that did not validate itself by works. My point, David, is this: Judaism is strong on works, but so were followers of Yeshua in the earliest Church. We agree on the importance of works; the issue is whether works in themselves justify, redeem or save; or if they validate, or vindicate the premise that faith is truly present. It is the latter I am wanting to stress to you.

In the same paragraph in which you discussed your understanding of the word 'saved', you state that all people are born 'intrinsically good'. David, are you saying that it is therefore theoretically possible for a person never to die? Then why *do* people die? Is it not because they sinned? Death would not have come into the world had Adam not sinned. But you are claiming that Cain and Abel were born intrinsically good. And yet it didn't take long before jealousy took over, did it (Gen. 4:5)? Where did this anger and jealousy come from? Surely it sprang from the fallen nature he inherited from his parents. So I am curious to know, since you aver that people today are born as Adam and Eve were created *before* the Fall, why is it always the case – no exceptions – that people sin and die? Surely, David, if you are correct, somebody one day among the billions of people that have been born would by now have proved your thesis that people are born intrinsically good. But all end up sinning, and all die. The one exception: Yeshua, who died – because the Lord laid on him all our iniquity – but was later raised to life for our justification (Rom. 4:25).

This is why the New Testament points to what came to be known as the doctrine of original sin, which you say you do not accept. You will know that Augustine put the position like this:

Posse pecare (able to sin) – that is, Adam and Eve before the Fall.

Non posse non pecare (not able not to sin) – that is, people after the Fall.

Posse non pecare (able not to sin) – that is, those who have faith in Christ.

Non posse pecare (not able to sin) – that is, once we are in Heaven.

Even if you lay aside Augustine and the New Testament, I would have thought that empirical evidence for people's predictability – they *always* sin sooner or later – suggests they must have been born with the propensity to sin. Where did this proclivity come from? I therefore suggest that we must go beyond the occasion they actually sin, when you say (if I understand you correctly) they qualify to be a 'sinner'. I would have thought the most reasonable explanation for sin in the world is what began in the Garden of Eden, and was then handed down to their offspring. Cain is surely Exhibit A.

To put it another way, I would love to know if the sages taught that Jesus departed from traditional Judaism when he defined sin as being in one's thoughts. As you know (and as I mentioned in a previous letter), Jesus taught that lusting is tantamount to committing adultery, hate is the equivalent to committing murder (Matt. 5:21–30). This is why Christians claim that all people are sinners and cannot keep the Law. If keeping the Law were merely *external*, one could say it is fairly possible to keep the first nine of the Ten Commandments. Saul of Tarsus felt comfortable in saying as much but admitted that, when he was gripped by the Tenth Commandment ('Thou shalt not covet'), he was a goner (Rom. 7:9–11). The teaching, therefore, that we are sinners because of the fallen nature we were born with, came from Jesus before Paul taught it. So where did Jesus go wrong?

I note that you believe Jesus was sincere but misguided. Your thoughts seem to parallel those of Albert Schweitzer, who claimed that Jesus hoped until the events portrayed in Matthew 11:20–24 that he would lead the nation from bondage to Rome, but then gave up that goal and became willing to die. You even suggest that Jesus might have conceived himself as the Messiah. But you do not think 'for one minute' that Jesus saw himself 'in terms of the theological construct that Christianity affirms'. I suppose by that you mean Jesus did not consciously believe he was the Son of God or that he believed he was *born to die* on a cross; that it was what the writers of the Gospels conceived. I suspect this is why a late date for the Gospels is important to your own interpretation – it gives more time for the earliest stories to be embellished. I reply: nobody in the earliest Church was clever enough to invent the resurrection of Jesus. Never – ever – would fishermen from Galilee have come up with the idea that Jesus died on the Cross for our sins, that he was raised from the dead and ascended to Heaven. It would have taken a thousand geniuses to create that idea!

The truth is, David, that the Twelve, or I should say the eleven disciples, to whom the resurrected Jesus appeared, did not have a clue why he died or why he was raised from the dead until the Holy Spirit fell on them on the day of Pentecost. It was the Holy Sprit who enabled them to see for the first time what Jesus' coming was all about.

I remember Rabbi Kellner's sole reason for not accepting Jesus as the promised Messiah: 'We still have wars. Messiah would bring peace.' You are saying much the same thing when you state that the Messiah the Jews eagerly awaited was a Messiah who would deliver them from Roman subjugation. But I would gently ask you to consider that, all along, God had something different in mind for Israel at that time. When Isaiah was given privy to this divine information, he wrote those words as if he trembled; he knew that his people would not be very happy about the kind of Messiah that he was going to describe.

Finally, you suggest I might be distinguishing between moral and ritual teachings because I said that messianic believers' holding to some Jewish rituals was good but not required. My answer: first, the morality that was required for the ancient people of God is eternal and unchanging. It is at this point, David, that you and I agree with each other wholeheartedly. The righteousness required by the Ten Commandments was regarded by the New Testament as the *minimum* standard of conduct for the believer in Jesus. But Jesus taught a righteousness of the *heart* that meant total forgiveness, no bitterness or hate, praying for enemies and doing righteous deeds without drawing attention to them. It is still an extension of the same Law of Sinai you uphold, only it goes beyond it, according to Jesus. This is why Jesus said that the kingdom of Heaven required a righteousness that 'surpasses' that of the Pharisees (Matt. 5:20). It was a righteousness that outclassed the letter of the Law.

Second, as for rituals, we believe that the Lord's Supper (sometimes called Eucharist – 'giving of thanks') is a fulfilment of Passover. It is also an important means of ensuring and promoting holiness (1 Cor. 11:27–32), thus the moral and ritual teachings come together in this particular ritual. This also means we keep Passover when we observe the Lord's Supper. As for the Sabbath, the issue is admittedly complicated. I blush to admit that we are generally divided on what is so clear to you. My relationship with you was born in the Shabbat meal you provided for us. The occasion was so moving it was almost enough to make me want to become an Orthodox Jew! Some Christians have held that the Sabbath is still the seventh day (beginning at sundown Friday). But most Christians slowly dropped the seventh day for the first day, very possibly because of anti-Semitic persecution but also to commemorate the resurrection of Jesus. But whether it was to be kept legalistically has been variously interpreted by the best of our theologians. I would understand if you think we are vulnerable here. For my own peace of mind I am satisfied with the words of Paul: 'One man considers one day more sacred than another; another man considers every day alike. Each one should be fully convinced in his own mind' (Rom. 14:5).

There is a reason, however, that Paul could say this. The Fourth Commandment is the *only* one of the Ten Commandments that is not quoted in the New Testament. This is because, as you say of the Fourth Commandment, which is replete with moral purpose and content, the Sabbath is ultimately fulfilled in the Sabbath rest of the *heart* that the Holy Spirit gives the people of God (Heb. 4:1–10). It is fulfilled not by what one does or does not do on a particular day of the week but by the soul resting in God. It promotes the very holiness Jesus envisaged when he talked about the standard required for the kingdom of Heaven. But I admit to you, I would not go to the stake for what I believe about the Sabbath.

Yours
RT

Letter 9

Dear RT

When I declare my reluctance to challenge you regarding your profession of faith, I am reflecting our fundamentally different attitudes towards one another.

You see me as condemned because I do not share your faith, whereas I do not see you as condemned because you do not share mine. I believe that you will go to Heaven if you lead a just and righteous life as God commands, whereas you do not believe that that will save me!

This fundamental difference in my approach to you leads me to acknowledge that I can never fully understand your faith conviction because I do not share/experience it. Therefore I cannot presume to empathise enough with it to properly question it. The idea that God is somehow exclusively incarnate in one human being is totally beyond my comprehension. The idea of the Trinity leaves me baffled. The concept of vicarious atonement defies my moral comprehension, and I could go on.

But the fact that I cannot empathise with these concepts does not lead me to presume to judge them or those who believe in them. I accept and respect the fact that you hold them sincerely, but I see no point in challenging you on them. In fact, it seems pointless to me to do so. I am content in my belief that there are different paths to God (to salvation) and ours are parallel paths united by common origins but profoundly divided by their development.

These parallel developments mean that we look back on our shared Scripture (that you call the Old Testament) and interpret it differently.

For me, it is obvious that Isaiah 53 refers to the children of Israel. Indeed, God's servant is referred to in various chapters of Isaiah categorically as 'my servant Jacob', 'Israel'. Isaiah 41:8–9 declares: 'And you, O Israel, are my servant; Jacob whom I have chosen; the seed of Abraham who loved me . . . You whom I have taken hold of from the ends of the earth; and I have said to you, You are my servant: I have chosen you and not spurned you.' Similarly, chapter 42, verses 1, 6 states: 'Behold my Servant Jacob whom I uphold; my elect in whom I delight . . . I have given you as a Covenanted people, as a light unto the nations'; chapter 43 verse 10 affirms: 'You are my witnesses, saith the Lord, and my Servant whom I have chosen'; and similarly chapter 44 verses 1, 2, 21 and 26, and chapter 45 verse 4.

Chapter 49 verse 3 starts out clearly referring to the same servant – 'You are my servant, Israel, in whom I will be glorified.' However, a fascinating process takes place in chapter 49, where Isaiah interchanges Israel and himself as the servant personifying the former and with the responsibility to preach for the former's sake and for the sake of all nations.

Otherwise, it seems to me to be most categorically clear that the servant is the people, Israel.

The basic message of the suffering of the servant in chapters 52 and 53, however, is understood by Jewish tradition to have profound theological meaning.

In brief, our understanding of what Isaiah is saying is that if one is chosen by God (whether one is worthy of such or not) to testify to the godly and the goodly in the world, then all that is hostile to the godly and the goodly will be hostile to you!

You will bear their sins, not in the sense of vicarious atonement (which contradicts Deuteronomy 24:16) but because their sinfulness will be thrust upon you – it will target you and in that sense you bear (have to bear up with) their sins!

We have also interpreted our own failures to live up to the high standard of the Sinai Covenant as part and parcel of the reason for our historic suffering; and that (in keeping with Amos (3:2)) being covenanted means not only the responsibility to live up to higher standards, but also to have to face more serious consequences for failure to do so. Of course, we knew that no matter how serious the consequences, divine love and promise would sustain us and eventually restore us to renew independent Jewish life in our ancestral homeland in keeping with Leviticus 26:44–5. Nevertheless, our own failures did not seem to be adequate enough an explanation for the enormity of Jewish suffering.

Isaiah's brilliant interpretation enabled us to see the hostility we encountered as something that had to be endured as part of being 'a light unto the nations', and as part of a process that would ultimately lead to the recognition on the part of evildoers of the perversion of their ways and inspire them and all humanity to walk along 'the path of righteousness for His Name's sake'.

Accordingly, Isaiah would not have been surprised by the fact that the might of the Nazi regime was so obsessed with the extermination of a small and weak people (even at the expense of Germany's own war effort!), because the Jewish nation embodies (through the eternal divine Covenant) everything that was the antithesis of the pagan, ungodly, power-obsessed bestiality of the Nazi regime. The latter thus found the very existence of even a 'Jewish embryo' to be intolerable!

To be God's servant is, of course, not just and not even primarily about suffering. It is, however, about standing for and standing up for the godly and the goodly, and this is our enormous honour but also, as a result, all too often our burden to bear.

Concluding my words about the identity of God's servant referred to by Isaiah, one might also note that all references to him are in the past tense (hundreds of years before the birth of Jesus.) It is interesting to note on this subject the words of the famous Christian Bible scholar O. C. Whitehouse, who comments on Isaiah chapters 52 and 53 (Century Bible) as follows: 'Christian exegetes should recognise that the path of Jewish exposition is in the main the right one and that the path of Christian interpreters down to the time of Rosenmuller have in the main been wrong.'

However, RT, I feel that Whitehouse has no right to say this to believing Christians (obviously he is entitled to his scholarly opinion), because what matters is the meaning people give to the text. If Christians like you want to read into it things that Jews like me do not believe are in the text, they have every right to do so.

The text thus acquires a different character and meaning for them and non-Christians should respect the meaning that Christians attribute to it – for them!

But to ask me to recognise a meaning that flows out of a faith that I do not have is – if you will forgive me saying so – both rather presumptuous and totally futile.

About Isaiah 9:6. This is not just a matter of seeing different meaning in the text, but also literally reading it differently.

The text refers to King Hezekiah, whose birth and ultimately his reign ushered in a new era for the Jewish people.

The verse should be read 'and he [Hezekiah] shall be called God the Mighty is Wonderful in Counsel, the Everlasting Father, Ruler of Peace' (Isa. 9:6, RSV). In other words, the description refers to God, and the child Hezekiah is given this additional name, to recall the Divine Presence and promise fulfilled in his reign. Indeed, the name Hezekiah itself means 'God is my strength' (and not that Hezekiah himself is the God of strength) and is similar to the meaning of the name of our second daughter, Gabriella. Calling people by names descriptive of divine actions and qualities is a most ancient Hebrew practice.

It seems to me to be precisely because we have such different theological perspectives (and perhaps also because I may not have explained myself adequately) that you are 'amazed to think that anybody could be saved by keeping the words of the Law!'

Let me reiterate, RT, that from my perspective there is nothing to be 'saved' from except our own failures, which we can always rectify because God in His unlimited mercy has given us the continuous capacity to reform ourselves and return to His path, His commandments.

Indeed, as God has revealed a higher and more religio-ethically demanding way of life to the children of Israel in the Sinai Covenant than that of the Noahide Covenant, I am saying that paradoxically it is easier for a Gentile to meet divine expectations. Again the word 'saved' might be misleading – I can only understand it in the sense of avoiding sin or reforming oneself from sinful ways.

In these regards it is obviously easier to avoid transgressing barely more than half a dozen commandments than a few hundred.

The word 'Law' is often portrayed by Christians in a negative light (following what I presume to consider to be a mistaken interpretation of Paul – at least mistaken in terms of the extent to which it is applied) as opposed to Love. In fact, I might point out in passing that the concept of love of God appears far more in the Hebrew Bible than the concept of fear of God. Because I reject the idea that there is some kind of dichotomy between love and Law, I prefer to avoid the latter term and thus its pejorative use. So, translating your comment, let me say, yes, RT, you are exempt from those additional commandments in the Sinai Covenant but not from those of the Noahide Covenant!

In keeping with the above, the way I understand the comment by Jesus that he had come to fulfil the Torah (which is translated as Law, but means the whole divine revelation at Sinai) is simply that he meant that he was a true and loyal Jew and had no intention of shirking his responsibility to live a life observing (fulfilling) the commandments of the Sinai Covenant – plain and simple!

In fact, I presume to state that the normative Christian understanding of Jesus' use of the word 'fulfil' seems strange to me. To me it seems obvious that to fulfil means to do everything one is expected to do, *not* to declare it unnecessary. Forgive me my impertinence, RT, but it seems to me that the Christian interpretation of what Jesus said actually turns his words on their head and interprets them to mean the opposite of what he had intended!

Naturally I see no connection between his final words on the Cross and the above.

Your question regarding death is similarly based upon an *a priori* perception of reality that is different from mine.

You assume that sin means death, but I do not. Sin is failure – a stumbling for which, yes, there are consequences, but not always death! Capital punishment is prescribed only for certain dire offences (though Rabbinic Judaism *de facto* virtually eliminated the death penalty through its demands regarding testimony for capital cases).

People die for the same reasons animals and vegetative life die – there is a biological cycle that is the natural order of the physical creation. But because humans are not only animals but are created in the Divine Image there is something eternal and imperishable within us that continues after our material being decomposes.

As far as the first narrative chapters of Genesis are concerned, I tend to share Maimonides' interpretation of them as allegorical with profound moral meaning. They are not, however, describing a biological reality. Certainly they warn us against disobedience against God. However, from the beginning of human existence we have always been physically perishable products!

I do not share your premise that it is even theoretically possible for anybody to avoid all sin, precisely because we have free choice. The fact that every human being has at some stage in his or her life stumbled and fallen does not prove that they are unable to stand firmly or run properly.

Let me reiterate – choice means by definition that sometimes we make mistakes. That is the meaning of the words in Ecclesiastes (7:20), 'for there is not a man on earth who does only good and never sins'.

In response to your question, RT, let me state that when Jesus taught that sin is already to be found in one's thoughts, he was indeed articulating Pharisaic teaching which declares much the same. Although the courts may not hold an individual culpable for such, our rabbis say that an individual *is* culpable for such before the Heavenly Court! Nevertheless, they would have been unlikely to have gone quite as far as to say that the thought of murder and adultery is actually the same thing as performing such terrible deeds.

Finally, I fully agree with you and Jesus that we have to go beyond the letter of the Law (in this case I'll allow myself to use that term) – in fact, the sages of the Mishnah and Talmud say that categorically. The medieval rabbinic authority Nachmanides (thirteenth century) put it eloquently when he described those who keep the letter of the Law but desecrate its spirit as 'knaves who function within the Torah's boundaries'.

But going beyond the letter of the Law does not mean to neglect the letter of the Law, let alone to desecrate it, God forbid. It means, for example, that it is not enough to avoid bowing down to graven images, but that you must not be subservient for example to money and greed. That, of course, doesn't mean that if you avoid the latter, it is all right to bow down and worship an idol!

I believe that those Pharisees whom Jesus was criticising were those who were obsessed with the letter at the expense of the spirit. Pharisaic rabbis of that time, and before and after, condemned such behaviour in no less harsh language, if not more so. They too required a higher righteousness, but not one that ignored the commandments; rather, they called for a higher righteousness that gives the practice of the commandments their full meaning and purpose, i.e. fulfils them!

Another example would be our sages' strong disapproval of prayer (a ritual of importance to both our traditions) when it is not motivated by true consciousness of the Divine Presence and appropriate intention.

In fact, Jewish mysticism devoted much attention and methods to increasing such consciousness and attention. However, any attempts to use this as an excuse for not observing the actual rituals was overwhelmingly derided and rejected.

I believe that it is a perennial human challenge to find the balance between form and substance, between structure and content. It is never an easy task. However, to reject form or structure because one has not found/experienced the appropriate substance and content is simply to throw out the baby with the dirty bathwater.

I believe that this is precisely the message that Jesus was bringing to 'the lost sheep of Israel', but it appears to me that those who took up his charge gave it a totally different meaning from that which he intended.

I have been less diplomatic than my usual self and I ask your forgiveness, RT, if anything I have said has in any way offended you.

Yours
David

Letter 10

Dear David

I reckon we must be getting things about right when each of us is apologising to the other for holding to staunch views and making statements with equal vigour. You, however, are truly a gentleman and a scholar and I doubt you are capable of being undiplomatic or ungracious.

I can understand your saying that my desire for you to recognise a meaning that flows out of a faith you do not have is 'both rather presumptuous and totally futile'. Presumptuous? Perhaps. Futile? I don't agree. All I am doing in these letters to you is what the Hebrew Scriptures call 'casting your bread upon the waters' (Eccles. 11:1).

You know that the essential issue between us is whether Jesus of Nazareth was and is the true Messiah that was promised to Israel. If he was not, then he was a fraud and every church spire in the world is a sepulchre to a dead God. But if in fact Jesus was raised from the dead and is truly the one and only Son of God, you have (it seems to me) lost everything, and will therefore know I am going to do my best to put the case to you and to do so for basically two constraining reasons: (1) it is my mandate from Jesus himself to urge you to become his disciple (Matt. 28:19); and (2) I want with all my heart to spend eternity in Heaven with you and your family.

On the first point, yes, I do have a command from Jesus. The Christian faith is essentially evangelistic. Like it or not, the very assumption that Jesus is 'the way, the truth and the life' and that no one comes to the Father apart from him (John 14:6) compels us to tell everybody the truth about him, especially our family and friends. It is not that we think we are a cut above others; we happen to take Jesus' words seriously and are required to tell all we meet that he is the Son of God, that his death on the Cross was and is God's way of salvation, and that those who do not hear and believe this message have no promise of Heaven.

On the second point, knowing as you do that I believe there is a Heaven and a Hell, and that only those 'in Christ' are assured of Heaven, what kind of friend would I be to you if I did not do all within my power to convince you? I am pleased to say that all my immediate family are 'born again' (to use Jesus' phrase to Nicodemus – John 3:3) and I would be thrilled no end to see this happen to you. When you said I see you as condemned if you do not share my faith, it did give me a slightly uneasy feeling that you suggest I am pointing the finger. But then I tell myself that you have the stature and magnanimity to know not to take it personally, since Jesus himself said: 'This is the verdict: Light [meaning himself] has come into the world, but men loved darkness rather than light . . .' (John 3:19). So please understand that I do not judge you in particular, David, because it was Jesus who said that he or she who does not believe in him is 'condemned already' (John 3:18).

Speaking of Nicodemus, a leading rabbi in his day, you will know that he was a secret believer in Jesus. Do you think there are any rabbis in Israel today that might be secret believers in

Jesus and believe in their hearts that he was Israel's Messiah and raised from the dead?

I personally think that, as I get to know you, you are as good as they come. I hope you discern that I really do mean this. But being good is not what saves us. If so, do you think a good Muslim could be in Heaven without acknowledging the true God? As for the Christian message of grace through faith, Emil Brunner called it the 'scandal' of the Gospel that we are saved by faith alone (apart from our demonstrating good works) in Christ alone.

I would, of course, be thrilled to see a leading Orthodox Jewish rabbi come to faith in Jesus as his Messiah. But what Christian wouldn't be thrilled? And yet I am being totally honest and blissfully candid when I tell you that I personally have no doubt that the day is coming that the nation of Israel (and Jews generally) as a whole will affirm that Jesus of Nazareth was and is God's promised Messiah after all – *before* he returns the second time. If my interpretation of Romans 11 is correct, this is guaranteed. How and when this will happen is to indulge in unprofitable speculation, but it is not unreasonable to assume that it could begin in earnest by somebody like you leading the way. I would give my very life for this to happen. So you should know that all I say as we write to each other is undergirded by the hope that God would use a dialogue like ours to ignite the flame that will blaze around the world.

What is my realistic hope that this might happen? It is because you are not only governed by integrity – a seeker and follower of truth wherever it leads – but also because you are as devoted to Holy Scripture as I am. You prove this by the way you defend your position *vis-à-vis* my own on passages like Isaiah 9:6 and Isaiah 53. You have taught me so much, not the least of which is how classic Judaism replies to the New Testament interpretation of the Torah and messianic prophecies (or what we believe to be messianic prophecies).

I would love to know whether you yourself believe that passages like Psalm 110, Isaiah 9:6 and Isaiah 53 *are* indeed messianic but some still unfulfilled. You have kindly replied regarding the way the sages have understood the latter two, but I am interested whether there are still in some sense unfulfilled prophecies that *you* hold to as you await your Messiah.

For example, you will know that Jesus asked your ancient people the Pharisees how they understood Psalm 110:1 ('The LORD said to my Lord: "Sit at my right hand until I put your enemies under your feet"') by asking: since David himself calls him 'Lord', how then can he be his son (Mark 12:36–7; cf. Matt. 22:44–5)? Our Gospels indicate that they could not answer Jesus. My question is: how do you think they should have answered him? And is there to be a priest 'in the order of Melchizedek' (Ps. 110:4) down the road, in your view? You will almost certainly know how our New Testament treats this in Hebrews 7, so I would hope to learn your way of handling this passage.

Thank you for bringing up the subject of the Trinity. I can understand your comment that the idea that 'God is somehow exclusively incarnate in one human being' as being totally beyond your comprehension. I cannot grasp this either. Who can? Your namesake King David could not fully take in the matter of God creating and loving humankind: 'What is man that you are mindful of him?' (Ps. 8:4) and felt much the same as he reflected on God's care and omniscience, 'Such knowledge is too wonderful for me, too lofty for me to attain' (Ps. 139:6). Our greatest hymn writer tried to put it into words:

> Let earth and heaven combine,
> Angels and men agree;
> To praise in songs divine

> The Incarnate Deity.
> Our God contracted to a span,
> Incomprehensibly made man.
>
> Charles Wesley (1707–88)

If we could fully comprehend such truths they would not be regarded as mysteries, neither would any of us need faith at all.

As for the Trinity, I am not about to tell you anything you don't know already, that we Christians do not remotely believe in three gods, for God is *one* (as in the *Sh'ma*): 'Hear O Israel: The LORD our God, the LORD is one' (Deut. 6:4). God is *one*, his Name is the Lord (or Yahweh, known to you as *HaShem*). His Son the Messiah is the very image and reflection of God and he touches us and speaks to us by his Spirit – the same Spirit who participated in creation (Gen. 1:2). The word 'Trinity' is not in the New Testament, as you know. Tertullian (c. 200) coined the Latin word *trinitas* and was the first of our Church Fathers to refer to the Father, Son and Spirit as *personae*. And yet I must tell you that one thing we are not willing to give up is the biblical teaching that God is one – it is not negotiable. Trinity is also an *a posteriori* explanation of our church fathers of how best to understand that God is manifest as Father, Son and Holy Spirit.

So if you are baffled, David, so am I. But I would prefer to use the word 'amazed'. To quote Charles Wesley again,

> Amazing love, how can it be?
> That Thou, my God, should die for me?

This reminds me of the first night we met – at your memorable Shabbat meal in Jerusalem, when we spontaneously sang together,

> Amazing grace, how sweet the sound
> That saved a wretch a like me!
> I once was lost, but now am found,
> Was blind but now I see.
>
> John Newton (1725–1807)

You no doubt believe that the Jews (in Israel and in the Diaspora) who have accepted Jesus as their Messiah are deceived. But would you go so far as to say they committed intellectual suicide? Some of the greatest minds in history, beginning with Saul of Tarsus, have crossed over from works to faith and did so with transparent integrity. Were you, David, to follow men like Nicodemus (John 3:1–10) and Joseph of Arimathea (John 19:38–42), you would *not* have to surrender your intellect or that brilliant mind the Lord gave you. For one thing you would not be baffled that God said, 'Let *us* make man in *our* image, in *our* likeness' (Gen. 1:26). The Hebrew Scriptures often use a plural noun (like *Elohim)* for God with a singular verb (like *bara* – created; Gen. 1:1). So after saying, 'Let us [plural] make man' come the words 'So God created [singular]'. The blueprint for what became known as the Trinity was imbedded in the very first chapter of Genesis. They are in harmony with Trinitarian beliefs and easily support them once a person crosses over the line from salvation by works to salvation by faith.

I was wondering why our belief in vicarious atonement defies your 'moral' comprehension. Where do you think we got the idea in the first place? From you! From the Torah, from the whole sacrificial system from Passover to the Day of Atonement. The blood was always required. Always. Without the shedding of blood there is no remission. 'For the life of a creature is in the blood, and I have given it to you to make atonement for yourselves on the altar; it is the blood that makes atonement for one's life' (Lev. 17:11). Works don't atone. Only blood. The word 'scapegoat' is even used regarding the Day of Atonement to show that sins have been transferred to a vicarious substitute (Lev. 16:8–10). The whole of the Epistle to the Hebrews is based upon the thesis that all that happened during the era of the sacrificial system (what we see as a 1,300-year parenthesis between the Law given through Moses at Sinai and Jesus' ascension to Heaven) begged – indeed, cried out – for fulfilment. Good works were then given a noble motivation; they were to be carried out in *gratitude* as opposed to their earning our way – which is very humbling. Were you, David, to make the Crossover to what I believe is the ultimate fulfilment of Passover, I think you better than anyone I have met could be the Number One Apologist for these things.

And if you think that the Christian faith is devoid of the place for works simply because we believe we are saved by Jesus' vicarious atonement for us, you have not been talking to the right persons. Though we are saved by grace through faith and not by works, we are none the less commanded to demonstrate good works (Eph. 2:8–10). I am sure you know the book of James well. You might be amused to know that one of my books – an exposition of James 1, 2 and 3 – is called *Justification by Works*. That we are saved by a vicarious sacrifice does not mean we are not called to moral purity and holiness of life. The opposite is true! 'By their fruit you will recognise' the true from the counterfeit, said Jesus (Matt. 7:20). As for my own definition of being saved, rather different from yours, I believe it refers in the main to being saved from the penalty of our sins: namely, eternal judgment.

Yes, we do differ as well on the result of the Fall of Adam and Eve. You say that I say sin means death; what I meant to convey is, death is the consequence of sin. So you are saying that Adam and Eve would have died even if God had not warned them in the Garden of Eden – that they would have died even had they not sinned. The orthodox Christian understanding is that their death came about *only because* they sinned.

Moving on to messianic prophecy, thank you for giving your interpretation of Isaiah 9:6. I agree that you have provided a plausible interpretation. All I would want to add is, should you one day affirm Jesus as the true Messiah, you would not have to make a giant leap but a mere side step to embrace the most natural, logical and grammatically sound translation of the verse – which I believe, of course, anticipates the incarnation: 'For a child has been born to us, a son has been given to us, and the government shall be on his shoulder, and his name is called Wonderful Counsellor, Mighty God, Father Forever, Prince of Peace.'

As for your point that Isaiah has described what already happened ('a child has been born') and therefore does not refer to the future, I had thought that this manner of speaking was done quite often in the Old Testament. For example, did not God tell Joshua that the land promised was already his (Joshua 1)? Even Rahab said to the spies, 'I know that the LORD has given this land to you' (Josh. 2:8). As for the destruction of Jericho, even before it was carried out, the Lord said to Joshua, 'See, I have delivered Jericho into your hands, along with its king and its fighting men' (Josh. 6:2). In much the same way, God called Gideon a 'mighty warrior' when he was a nobody, if not a coward (Judg. 6:12). God sees the end from the beginning (Isa. 46:10) and I would have thought that he can speak prophetically that something has already happened when in fact it is still future.

You make a good case, David, that the suffering servant of Isaiah is Israel. But is this the entire explanation? I would welcome you to sit down with me (so to speak, since we are some 6,000 miles apart) and devote a future letter to Isaiah's messianic prophecies alone. I would be interested if your point of view (that it is always a reference to a nation and not to a single man) will bear a scholarly scrutiny. I will go there if you will. Speaking personally, I would be willing for our entire dialogue to hinge on what Isaiah envisages, especially chapter 53. I could start this journey right now but would prefer to hear you say, 'Yes, RT, I want to examine these passages with you.'

As for your interpretation of the reasons Jews are persecuted, I was very moved – and persuaded. You state that 'all that is hostile to the godly and the goodly will be hostile to you!' Yes. And the people of Israel, whether in the land of Israel or in eastern Europe, have suffered too because they are, simply, chosen by God. The hatred that some people throughout the world feel towards Jews is largely traceable, in my opinion, to the very *fact* of God's word to Moses, 'I will have mercy on whom I will have mercy' (Exod. 33:19), such people being the seed of Abraham, Isaac and Jacob.

I happened to be in England last week on the sixtieth anniversary of the liberation of Auschwitz, also Holocaust Memorial Day. I wanted to fly to Poland. I don't know if I have told you, but I visited Auschwitz in June 1974. I will never forget it as long as I live. The word 'horrible' doesn't even come close to how awful it was. I would have liked to be there last week, if only to do my part in apologising to the Jewish people of this world for what was done – partly in the name of so-called 'Christianity'.

Louise and I attended the play *Fiddler on the Roof* in New York a few months ago. I wept as it ended, and tears rolled down our faces as we walked out, knowing not only how much Jewish people have suffered but that the persecution goes on and on. But seeing the play did, if anything, give me a greater love for Jewish people, and also the land of Israel.

I was just a little disquieted when you wrote in your last letter that all roads lead to God – or have I wrongly paraphrased your statement 'there are different paths to God (to salvation)'?

I had assumed that as an Orthodox Jewish rabbi, even if you offer the Noahide Covenant as a non-Jewish way of salvation, you would at least require that all people bend the knee to Yahweh – the God of the Bible. When you refer to the scholar who wrote in the Century Bible that a particular Jewish explanation for Isaiah 53 is the best one, you realise, don't you, that there are those within the circumference of the Christian community who do not believe at all that Jesus is the only way? Such people have departed from the orthodox Christian faith just as some of your people have deserted the Torah. I thought this conviction – that Yahweh alone is the true God and has revealed himself infallibly in his Torah – was partly what made an Orthodox Jew an Orthodox Jew! And yet you surely would not say that Jesus is an acceptable path to God – or would you? Or perhaps there is in you, David, a liberal spirit that allows you to be very orthodox and very liberal at the same time. If this is the case (which I suspect) it is no doubt why you would enter into dialogue with me in the first place – and I am therefore so grateful. But on the other hand, my hope in seeing you come to affirm Jesus as your Messiah is mostly grounded in our common belief – in the full inspiration of the Hebrew Scriptures. This is why I am prepared to go into detail with you on Isaiah 53.

I think I am saying that my hope in these conversations with you, as I have candidly written from the first day, is based on our high view of Scripture. I have great confidence in seeing you make the Crossover if we carefully examine Scripture, but I am less hopeful if you really do believe that all paths lead to salvation. But, David, I will not give up on you, even if the latter turns out to be the case. Why? First, you are a man made in the Image of God and I believe you need what I have, namely a heart-to-heart relationship with your Messiah, Jesus. Second, you are the *natural* olive tree that I have referred to before, and it will take little effort (if I may put it like that) by the Holy Spirit to bring you to the acceptance of the Messiah that I embrace. I pray for you daily, admire you very much and feel I am singularly honoured to have this relationship with you. I doubt this happens to many people and I only want to do my very best to fulfil Jesus' command to me.

I wish most of all that you feel love from me. If you don't, I have utterly failed and let my Lord down. It is easy for an argument or proposition to take over and camouflage the love I really do feel for you. So if I have pressed you too hard again, thank you for forgiving me again! May I end this letter with the lovely benediction that closed your last one, with love and blessings *to you and to the land and the city that is dear and holy to us both.*

Yours
RT

Letter 11

Dear RT

It seems that with all our mutual respect and affection, our conversation is now getting a little polemical and that probably is inevitable.

Let me begin my response to the main thrust of your last letter by telling you a personal story.

I came to interfaith relations as a result of my religious commitment to social justice. When I was rabbi of the largest Jewish congregation in South Africa more than twenty-five years ago, I sought to do something to counteract the iniquitous governing system of racial separation known as *apartheid*. One of the few ways one could bring people together across racial lines without automatically antagonising the government and getting oneself thrown into jail or out of the country was through religious meetings. So I founded the Inter-Faith Forum – a council of Christians, Jews and Muslims – in order to enable communities to become better acquainted with one another first of all by bringing religious leaders together.

I hawked my wares around with the same opening gambit: 'You know, Reverend, Father, Imam, Sheikh, Rabbi, the things that should bring us together are more important than the things that keep us apart,' and they all concurred and agreed to be part of this initiative. However, in the South African context I knew that if I did not involve the Dutch Reformed Church in South Africa, the enterprise was of limited value. The ruling party at that time was the Afrikaner Nationalist Party, and the Dutch Reformed Church was often referred to as the 'Nationalist Party at prayer'!

In the demonology of the South African Dutch Reformed Church, there were two famous perceived threats – one was 'the black threat' and the other was 'the Catholic threat'.

I learned that a Dominee – a Dutch Reformed minister – in downtown Cape Town was involved in dialogue with Catholics. So I thought, well if he talks to Catholics maybe he'll talk to Jews as well! I arranged to meet him and after exchanging pleasantries I repeated my opening gambit which had worked so well until then. 'You know, Dominee,' I said, 'the things that join us together are more important than the things that keep us apart.' To my surprise he answered me, 'To tell you the truth, Rabbi, I cannot agree with you. The most important thing in my life keeps us apart. That is my belief in Jesus as my personal Saviour. You do not share that, Rabbi, and I have to tell you the truth, that you will go to Hell because you do not share that faith! And it is my duty to try to save you from going to Hell. So the only reason for me to meet with you is to save you from that fate!'

Naturally I was a bit taken aback, but I said something that I don't know if I fully believed then but do now believe very much. I said, 'Well, thank you for your honesty, Dominee. I still would like you to come along to our meetings and you will have your opportunity to try and convert me. But I think it is important anyway that I learn to understand you better and that you learn to understand me better.' And indeed he did come to our meetings and became less doctrinaire and, I believe, more understanding of others' beliefs. He also brought in other Dutch Reformed ministers to our gatherings.

This was an important lesson for me. First, not to react negatively to missionary claims or proselytising initiatives (as opposed to most of my co-religionists – an attitude I will try to explain below), but above all to always encourage the human encounter that can enrich and broaden one's own outlook and that of others.

I often refer to Bishop Krister Stendahl (former Presiding Bishop of Sweden) who articulated three ground rules for interfaith dialogue: first, always try to understand others as they understand themselves; second, try to view other faith communities by the best within them (and not the worst); and finally, leave room for 'holy envy'. It's nice when we can say, 'That's just like what we do, or we believe,' but one should not feel the need to be reticent about admiring something in another faith that might not be part of one's own tradition. There need be nothing disloyal to one's own heritage in viewing something with admiration in another tradition.

Getting back to the point, however. My reaction to being seen as an object for proselytisation is not typical. The overwhelming majority of Jews find this to be highly offensive. To begin with, it is seen as disrespectful to our own Jewish integrity because it implies that our Jewish heritage – the faith of the patriarchs and the prophets of the Hebrew Bible – is deficient and flawed. However, it also conjures up for the Jew the whole tragic history of the 'teaching of contempt' of Christendom towards Jews and Judaism that produced a theology not only of supercessionism but also of condemnation and persecution of the Jew. It is important, RT, that you, and all Christians who share your world view, should know how distressing and offensive most Jews find any attempt to proselytise them.

I personally am fully aware of the fact that not only do you feel duty bound to try to do this, but you actually feel that it would be wrong to desist from doing so. I cannot argue with you over this. I can only try to make you aware of how painful this is to most Jews and to suggest that in the shadow of all the terrible things that have been done to the Jewish people down the course of history, ostensibly in the name of Christianity, you might actually owe it to your own faith to rehabilitate its tragically negative image in the minds and hearts of so many of the nation into which Jesus was born.

Forgive me for making the point even more brutally. It must surely be a scandal for you that the very name of Jesus, who saw himself as a loyal son of Israel, still generates such negative reactions among the Jewish people. This, as you have acknowledged, is the result of the tragic experience of Jews at the hands of so-called Christians throughout the centuries. However, if sincere Christians today want Jews to react to the name of Jesus with respect and admiration, then Jews need to feel that Christians respect *them* for who and what they are. The overwhelming majority of Jews will never feel that that is the case as long as they perceive that they are being told they are deficient and condemned. To me, RT, it seems that you are caught between what you see as your evangelical duty and your responsibility to honour the very name through which you pray!

You imply that it is completely compatible to be a believer in Jesus and still remain a Jew. I would say this depends upon who and what you believe Jesus is. For those who maintain that Jesus is the Messiah, as I have indicated previously, I fail to understand this claim in the face of the unfulfilled conditions of the Messianic Age as envisioned in the writings of the Hebrew prophets. However, I would not for a minute suggest that one cannot be a Jew and hold such a belief. As I may have mentioned, there is a Hassidic sect today that believes that its rabbi, who died a few years ago, is the Messiah and will reveal himself as such when the time is ready. No one (or hardly anyone) suggests that they cannot be considered faithful Jews as a result.

Indeed, a century after Jesus' death, arguably the greatest rabbi of all, Rabbi Akiva, believed that Simon Bar Coziba (known as Bar Cochba – Son of a Star) was the Messiah: that he would throw off the yoke of Rome (which he actually did for a few years!), ingather the exiles, establish a rule of justice and righteousness and usher in an era of universal peace. However, Bar Cochba did not succeed in bringing about the Messianic Age that the Jews so yearned for. On the contrary: his defeat led to even more Jewish suffering as the Romans intensified their persecution, executing large numbers including the religious leaders of the Jewish people – Rabbi Akiva among them.

In all probability, Nicodemus and other Jews who believed that Jesus was the Messiah had similar expectations. When these were not realised, they either gave up on the idea or reinterpreted it, as did Christianity.

I, RT, am personally more generous than you appear to expect non-Christians to be regarding their perception of Christianity. I respect Christianity's reinterpretation of the Messianic idea according to its own conviction and I myself would not claim that Jesus or his followers who reinterpreted this idea were frauds. Rather, I view them as the progenitor and adherents of a new religion that was and is something quite different from the Judaism from which it sprang.

Accordingly, if Jews believe in the fundamental Christian concepts of the Incarnation, the Salvific Sacrifice of the Crucifixion and the Trinity, if they are truthful they will acknowledge that these ideas are incompatible with normative Jewish teaching. If Jews believe in these concepts, they should at least honestly identify themselves as Christians.

As we have noted before, we Jews and Christians interpret our shared Bible differently. I am not concerned here with biblical criticism but with explaining how Rabbinic Judaism interprets biblical texts. From a traditional Jewish viewpoint sacrificial rites could not atone for sins in themselves unless they reflected sincere contrition in the heart of the sinner, which would be articulated accordingly. Thus the prophet Hosea says (14:1–2), 'Return, O Israel, unto the Lord your God for you have stumbled in your transgression. Take with you *words* and return unto the Lord your God. Say unto Him, take away all iniquity and accept us graciously; so *we will render as bullocks the offerings of our lips.*' Similarly the prophet Joel declares (2:13), 'Rend your heart and not your garments and turn unto the Lord your God; for He is gracious and full of compassion, slow to anger and plenteous in mercy and forgives iniquity.' Our ancient sages affirm that 'there is no atonement without repentance' (Mishna Yoma 8:8), that 'sincere repentance and works of loving kindness [charity] are the real intercessors before God's throne' (TB Shabbat 32a) and that 'sincere repentance is the equivalent to the rebuilding of the Temple, the restoration of the altar and the offering of *all* the sacrifices' (TB Sanhedrin 43b). In terms of Jewish understanding of the sacrificial rites in the Temple, while the blood of the sacrifice did indeed represent life, it was seen precisely in a representational role symbolising 'the complete yielding up of the worshipper's life to God' (J. H. Hertz, *Pentateuch and Haftorahs*, Soncino Press, 1986, p. 487).

Indeed, following on from the sages' affirmation that Temple offerings were only of value as an outward manifestation of an internal condition, the medieval Jewish scholars Maimonides and Don Isaac Abravanel (the latter basing himself on an ancient Midrash, or rabbinic homily, on Leviticus 17:7) viewed the whole sacrificial order as only a concession to the form of worship that was common and expected at the time of the Sinai revelation. They taught that the biblical sanction of this form of religious service was precisely designed to wean the

people away from the prevailing primitive methods of idol-
atrous worship at the time. In keeping with our sages' teaching
on the power of sincere repentance and prayer, these scholars
believed that after the destruction of the Temple, the sacrificial
rites had been replaced by a higher form of divine worship,
that of prayer.

Bottom line, RT: Rabbinic Judaism does not accept the
idea of vicarious sacrifice. We can only atone for our own sins
and are responsible for our own actions.

Regarding your questions about Psalm 110, it is actually
not clear to me from the passages in Matthew and Mark as to
exactly what the point was that Jesus was making. Simply read,
it would appear to me that he is saying that the Messiah cannot
be the son of David, but must be David himself! That seems to
me to be a very interesting interpretation of the text and I can
quite understand how Jesus' brethren may have felt that he had
made a convincing argument.

I, however, would point out that the English translation of
the verse in Psalm 110 is a little misleading. The same word,
'Lord', appears twice for two different words in the Hebrew
version. They are the Tetragrammaton – the four-lettered name
of God, YHWH – and *adoni*, which simply means 'sire'! Now
it is true that this latter word can be used in the highest
reference to God Himself, but it is also used all the way down
the human social scale as a courteous address to a stranger. My
understanding (and the traditional Jewish understanding) of
the Psalm is that it is portraying God's special love and 'respect'
for David (in whose name the psalm is written). In this light, it
would be perfectly logical to understand the word *adoni* as
simply indicating this special divine regard and endearment
for David.

Indeed, Psalm 110 *was* given messianic allusion by some,
precisely in relation to David and his lineage. Personally though,
I'm not convinced that this was its original meaning and am

more inclined to accept the view that the original intent of the text was to confirm the special place of the Davidic household.

To be sure, there are Psalms and many passages in Isaiah that are of messianic portent, though I do not consider Isaiah 9:6 and Isaiah 53 to be such. I do not accept your claim that the language in the latter can be compared to the references you give from Joshua, which in fact are expressions of imminent anticipation of events that are then subsequently described.

As far as your desire, RT, to enter into these texts in greater depth, I am perfectly willing to do so. However, I have my doubts as to the value of this. I think it is already pretty clear how and why we will give our different interpretations.

You are probably correct in your suggestion that my religious pluralist outlook is not typical of most Orthodox rabbis. I should point out that 'Orthodox' was not a word that observant religious Jews chose to describe themselves. It was actually borrowed from Christianity by Reform Jews to describe those Jews who remained doggedly attached to traditional Jewish practice. A more appropriate word to describe what is called Orthodoxy (meaning correct belief) is 'orthopraxis' (meaning correct behaviour). Judaism has always been able to tolerate a variety and differences of opinion on matters of belief (although obviously within certain limits). Where it has demanded consensus has been with regard to the observance of the commandments – the practice of the Jewish way of life.

As far as my own theological outlook is concerned, of course I believe that there is only one God, Creator and Guide of the Universe. But it seems obvious to me that just as He has created us and relates to us in all our diversity, so there are diverse ways of recognising and relating to Him. Indeed I do *not* deny the Christian's choice of Jesus as his or her path to God. In fact I believe, in keeping with many of our greatest medieval sages (notwithstanding their suffering at the hands of so-called

Christians), that the mystery of the Christian faith has enabled the truths of biblical revelation to be extended to a vast portion of humanity, thereby sanctifying the Name of the One God.

I do not, however, believe that any one religious tradition can encapsulate the totality of the divine. Indeed, I consider such a claim to be something of an impiety. I realise, RT, that you do not share this view and that you feel an obligation to convince me that what you believe is the exclusive truth. As I have said, I am confident enough in both my own faith and my pluralist theology not to feel threatened by this. Moreover, I am fortunate that I myself do not consciously bear the scars, let alone open wounds, of Jewish history (even very recent history) that make others among my co-religionists react differently.

However, I continue this dialogue with you not out of any illusion that either of us will change in our commitments (for which, as I say, I have no desire – on the contrary), but out of the conviction that the more we understand one another, the better it is for us, our communities and our world – and the more we are likely to fulfil the will and purpose of our Father in Heaven whose Name we seek to hallow.

I pray that we may each be worthy of this charge and that this goal may be achieved through respect for every person and each community's integrity.

Yours
David

Letter 12

Dear David

If our dialogue has become 'a little polemical' I hope this is not necessarily a bad thing. You kindly say this was probably inevitable, but I fear that I am chiefly responsible for this. But your expression did give me pause. At some point in our exchanges I think I began playing 'hard ball', as we say over here, rather than soft ball – a safer, slightly slower sport I enjoyed as a boy in Kentucky. I prefer watching hard ball (baseball, the American pastime) but I always preferred playing soft ball. I wasn't cut out for hard ball. But I do thank you that you responded exactly as you did.

However, I am now wondering, David, for my own part, if I should play soft ball from now on. I do not intend to hurl a fast ball or a curve, and I never intend to put you on the spot. If it should seem that way I can assure you I am trying to learn from you as well as to write in a manner that is consistent with the agreed purpose of our correspondence – not to mention my obedience to Jesus' command.

You write with a compassionate heart for your people and express the hope that I might be aware of how painful it is to most Jews to be the 'object for proselytisation'. To be honest, I don't think I was aware of this at all – until your last letter. I don't think I realised how highly offensive some of us – including me – have been. Not that I myself have had this kind of interchange with Jewish people all that often. I told you earlier about my conversations with Rabbi Abraham Kellner and Nathan Darsky. As far as I can recall, I can remember only one Jewish person – a lady named Luba from Moscow – who accepted Jesus (as a consequence of my street ministry), and I did not know for several years that she was in fact Jewish. You therefore lovingly challenge me 'to rehabilitate' the negative image in the minds and hearts of so many Jewish people that has been put there in the name of so-called Christianity. I want to do that as best as I can.

I hope you already know this, but let me say it emphatically: I do have a warm love and respect for the Jewish people, and I am thoroughly ashamed of what has been perpetrated on them by the so-called 'Christian' Church over the centuries. How can you forgive us? Israel, both the land and God's special people, has a unique place in God's heart and also his purposes, particularly in these end-times. (Yes, I really do believe we are in the end-times.) And many – and rapidly increasing numbers of – believers in Jesus are experiencing a heartfelt love for Israel and the Jewish people. I sincerely apologise for having allowed my own zeal to have too much rein.

I should add that our mandate from Jesus to 'go into all the world' and preach the gospel to every human being (Mark 16:15) does not imply that any one group of people are any more deficient or flawed than another, and certainly not God's historic Covenant people. 'The LORD looks down from heaven on the sons of men to see if there are any who understand, any who seek God. All have turned aside, they have together become corrupt; there is no one who does good, not even one,' as King David said 3,000 years ago (Ps. 14:2–3). Again,

'No one living is righteous before you' (Ps. 143:2). And yet surely the *least* flawed or *least* deficient (using your words) *should* be Jewish people because of their heritage and 'head start' in knowing God's Word and God's ways. Therefore any attempt on my part in talking to someone like you about receiving Jesus as your Messiah does not for one second imply that I see you – or any Jewish person – as particularly deficient or flawed as human beings. I just regret – and apologise – that so many of us have failed in making this clear.

On the other hand, I must say, with greatest respect, I believe your *belief system* is flawed. Otherwise the people of Israel generally 2,000 years ago would have embraced their Messiah. And I should add that *all* people – not just Jewish people – are offended by efforts of the Church to evangelise. I did it every Saturday morning right in front of Westminster Chapel in Buckingham Gate for almost twenty years. I talked with thousands and thousands and gave away countless pieces of literature in possibly fifty languages. *Nobody* cheered at first when we offered them a pamphlet or asked questions about their assurance of going to Heaven if they were to die that day.

By the way, thank you for making it clear that you yourself are not offended by people talking to *you* about these things. I think this is brilliant. But when I first read your last letter, having just returned from London and in a bit of jet-lag, I hastily thought you were saying 'leave us alone', including yourself. And I thought, 'Oh dear, what have I done and what do I do now?' I certainly felt better when I re-read your letter the next day. And I can *truly* understand if you really do hope in your heart that Christians will leave Jewish people alone. Such Christians are not likely to do so, even if our correspondence is read by them around the world, but I do pray that I myself will apply your timely caution in a manner that will be appropriate and dignifying to the Name I hold dear.

I know you absolutely did not mean for me to feel

uncomfortable or feel the slightest sting when you referred to the Dutch Dominee. And yet the way you quoted him could be a paraphrase or summary of what I happen to believe about the need for anyone to accept Jesus. 'Comparisons are odious', as Shakespeare said, and I do not believe you were comparing me to the Dominee. But as Jewish people are sensitive about Christians trying to convert them, I too am sensitive – no doubt too sensitive – in this matter of sometimes being lumped with certain empty-headed Bible-belt people, a number of them being racists, who believe the Scriptures – 'from Genesis in the front to maps in the back', as some put it. Although never judged like this by you, David, I am at times in the awkward position of being lambasted and compared to fundamentalist Muslims and even ultra-Orthodox Jews. Some go as far as to say the root cause of evil in the world is religious people like this.

I am a strong evangelical, I do indeed believe that all people – whoever they are – need to be saved, am fully convinced of the infallibility of the Scriptures and of my reformed theology. But I *too* believe in social justice. And I have always sought friends and fellowship in and outside the Christian Church with those who have different theological and political views from my own. Moreover, I led our church in Fort Lauderdale to have combined worship with a black church nearby – and that was in the 1960s. As for South Africa, you would be delighted to know that my teaching on James 2:14ff (the need for faith to be accompanied by works if that faith is to make an impact) had such an effect on Dr Michael Eaton, who was pastor of a church on the edge of Soweto, that he opened his church to black people and claims that my ministry changed his life and direction from then on. I might add that my wife Louise began praying daily for Nelson Mandela during the last twelve years he was in prison. And she has continued praying for him every day since.

You and I really do have a lot in common. As you are not a typical orthodox Jewish rabbi – and probably get not a little criticism from your fellow rabbis – so I know what it is to be isolated and warned against by Reformed ministers. But if I have tried a little bit too hard in our mutual exchanges, I ask for your forgiveness. My theology teaches that only God can save and that every person receiving Jesus is the result of the sovereign work of the Holy Spirit, but sometimes I still move ahead of the Lord and foolishly try to do his work for him! Let me say again: know assuredly, David, that I see nothing flawed or deficient in you as a person. I have no doubt that you are as good as they come. But at the same time I believe that all men and women on the planet need the Saviour who gave his life for the world 2,000 years ago – then rose from the dead.

You will almost certainly know that the resurrection of Jesus from the dead is the linchpin of all I believe. He really did rise from the dead! Furthermore, his death vindicated all he *said*, all he *claimed* for himself and all he *did* when he died vicariously for our sins on the Cross. He was the fulfilment of all that sacrificial system pointed to. Is it not interesting also that his death coincided perfectly with Passover? Had Jesus not been raised from the dead, all I believe is worthless. But since he did indeed come forth from the tomb on that first day of the week 2,000 years ago, I must take seriously all that is said about him in the New Testament – including his final words to his disciples before he ascended to Heaven, namely, to make disciples of everybody we meet!

I still say that it is indeed completely compatible for you to be a believer in Jesus and remain a Jew. I have to add, a very good Jew indeed. I have no doubt whatever that you could do this without violating what is written in the Law, the prophets and the writings. I detect a difference, however, between what was *written* in the Torah and what you believe was the *sitz im leben* (life situation) at the time of Sinai that gave us the Torah.

You did not comment on whether accepting Jesus would be committing intellectual suicide for you. If you are convinced indeed that the sacrificial system was a big mistake, then, yes, you would commit intellectual suicide by embracing vicarious atonement. But if you defended what is *written* in the Torah, you could accept Jesus with utter integrity and become one of the greatest apologists for the faith of Jesus in 2,000 years. Would I be wrong, David, in surmising that embracing the Torah as it is *written* would be almost as great a leap for you as accepting Jesus himself?

But what discourages me most, therefore, is not merely that you apparently do not believe in the concept of vicarious sacrifice; it is that you imply that the whole sacrificial system was ill-posed by Moses from the beginning. It was, you say, 'a concession to the form of worship that was common and expected at the time of the Sinai revelation'. This may be your conclusion but, in my opinion, it is the conclusion also of medieval Jewish scholars (whom you quote) who in my opinion lost heart about what Judaism once took for granted. I take the view that a disillusionment with the sacrificial system began to set in shortly after Jesus died, and most certainly after the Temple was destroyed some forty years later.

As for Maimonides, did he not disagree with Rabbi Rashi in the eleventh century over the latter's departing from norma-tive rabbinic thinking? Was not Rashi's interpretation of Isaiah 53 regarded as novel in 1050 when he claimed that the prophet was referring to the suffering of the nation of Israel because of the Gentiles? Is it not true that for centuries rabbis virtually without exception had seen Isaiah 53 as describing *not* the suffering of Israel but the Messiah himself? Rabbi Jonathan ben Uzziel's Targum (first century) of Isaiah 52:13 ('My servant will act wisely; he will be raised and lifted up and highly exalted') implied this when he wrote, 'My Servant Messiah shall prosper.'

I admit to skating on thin ice when I quote authorities like these men to *you*, David! It would be like you correcting my theological understanding by quoting John Calvin! But did not Maimonides write that *since the Temple no longer exists*, and there is therefore no atonement altar, nothing is left but repentance; hence 'repentance atones for all transgression'? In other words, since there is no altar or most holy place, repentance alone would have to suffice.

I thought that the ancient prophets called on Israel to repent *and* offer the sacrifices from a true heart – not to repent *instead* of offering the sacrifices. But because of statements in Hosea 6:6 ('For I desire mercy, not sacrifice', a verse Jesus was fond of quoting; Matt. 9:13, 12:7), were there not developing ideas which had been around since the Babylonian exile and the development of the synagogue and the home as an alternative to Temple worship? It seems to me that this development ultimately came into its own once the medieval rabbis diverted from the way earlier rabbis had viewed Isaiah 53.

As for the prophets calling for observance of the sacrifices *with* a true heart, this is exactly what Paul meant in Romans 1:17 by the righteousness (or justice) of God being revealed 'from faith to faith' (KJV). Had Paul not put it that way one could infer that Karl Barth was right when he claimed that Jesus not only died for everybody without exception but even believed for us; that all were saved by the death and faith of Jesus whether they believed it (or even knew about it) or not. But faith being *joined* by faith meant that the faith of *Jesus* which was saving had to be *ratified* by *our* own faith in order for the atonement of the Cross to be made effectual. I am trying to show, David, that vicarious atonement as taught in the New Testament is *not* effectual without our faith and repentance.

In my personal devotional reading this very morning, I read where Jesus told the Pharisees of his day, 'You have let go of the commands of God and are holding on to the traditions of men' (Mark 7:8). (The issue at that moment was not the sacrificial system but the Fifth Commandment.) When you said that the 'bottom line' is that Rabbinic Judaism does not believe in vicarious atonement, I was wondering who you are speaking for. All rabbis? All orthodox rabbis today? All rabbis for the last 2,000 years? Surely not the rabbis in the era that preceded the time of Jesus, or have I missed it here? In other words, are you saying that Rabbinic Judaism has by universal consensus *changed* from what it used to be? Is this kind of reinterpretation of the Torah – or adding to it – not the very thing Jesus was concerned about with the Pharisees of his day? If so, is this an inherent characteristic or tenet of Pharisees, to reinterpret as they go along? Is not the Law unchanging?

I take it that you don't like it very much when Jews who do accept Jesus refer to themselves as 'messianic believers' rather than Christians. You want them to call themselves Christians – full stop. Surely the Jewish people who embrace Jesus are wanting to demonstrate that their belief is most certainly not a 'new religion … quite different from the Judaism from which it sprang' but the fulfilment and ultimate reason for the Torah in the first place.

I agree with you that people like Nicodemus and other Jews who believed that Jesus was the Messiah had expectations of Rome being overthrown and the former glory of Israel being restored. Not only Nicodemus, but every single one of Jesus' disciples. Even *after* Jesus' death and *after* his resurrection (but before the Ascension) the disciples who were closest to him still anticipated the very kind of Messianic Age you and most Jews still look for if the true Messiah does appear. When Jesus was asked, 'Are you at this time going to restore the kingdom to Israel?' he replied, 'It is not for you to know the times or dates the Father has set by his own authority' (Acts 1:6–7). He then promised the power that would come on them (which did indeed happen on the day of Pentecost). It was no doubt a major shift and radical adjustment as to what the Messiah would be like and do, that Jews then and now have to make when they accept Jesus as their Messiah. On this point we agree.

By the way, may I ask what kind of Messiah you really do envisage? Do you think he is going to appear soon? How would you and all the Jewish people recognise him?

Thank you for giving me your view of Psalm 110:1. That is very interesting. If I may give my opinion on the point Jesus was making regarding Psalm 110, I take the view that he was showing that immediately after the Messiah's ascension into Heaven, when Jesus would take his place at the right hand of God, *Yahweh* (God the Father) would say to *Adonai* (the Son), 'Sit at my right hand until I make your enemies a footstool for your feet.' I would be delighted to elaborate on this if you like, but perhaps you feel this would have the equivalent value you envisage if we more fully explored Isaiah 53. I will not push either Isaiah or Psalm 110 on you. But even if you differ with the way Jesus interpreted Psalm 110:1, and although you vehemently disagree with it, will you not concede that Matthew's *redaction* was designed to prove that Jesus the Messiah was also the Son of God (Matt. 22:41–6)?

When I was at seminary over thirty years ago, I was introduced to the thinking of men like Rudolf Otto (*The Idea of the Holy*) and Adolf Harnack, who also saw a common denominator that was valid and authentic if not unifying in all the religions of the world. I suspect most of the students at the time (so it seemed) embraced this type of thinking with both arms. But I did not, for some reason. Had I done so, you and I, David, would not be having this challenging dialogue. Most of them became either universalists, annihilationists, existentialists or all the above. Some of them left the ministry they had come to train for, since they came to regard the Bible as a faulty and unreliable document and saw no reason to uphold the faith they once thought they believed. I was exposed to the same evidence they had examined, I read the same books they read and explored the same higher criticism of the biblical documents that so many of my friends took on board. I cannot tell you why I did not develop as they did. But here I am, now in my seventieth year, and I can look back with incalculable gratitude to God for preserving me from the heterodoxy that enthralled these old friends of mine.

I close by asking you once again: please forgive me for my zeal. Thank you, David, for teaching me so much, especially showing me that I must maintain a more tender spirit and empathetic understanding towards Jewish people, and helping me to grasp your pain and theirs when people like me push the boat out too far.

Yours
RT

Letter 13

Dear RT

As you know, in the past a polemical debate had more negative connotations than it necessarily has today. Nevertheless I still feel that there is something futile in it — a kind of 'he said, she said' quality. Indeed, I myself relate to these kinds of discussions with a degree of what one might call tolerant resignation. But as I sought to make clear in my last letter, as far as the overwhelming majority of the Jewish people is concerned, the attitude of 'leave us alone' and 'get off my back' precisely reflects their feelings and attitudes towards missionary activity. With all the genuine love in the world, a proselytising approach on the part of Christians will always mean tensions with the Jewish community and will never result in any kind of collective mutual respect. Our personal relationship, RT, is very much an exception to the rule, and I reiterate that while I personally respect your beliefs, as opposed to you I am a pluralist (although not a relativist) and do not believe that there is one exclusive path to God (and again reiterate that I find that idea something of an impiety — implying in fact a 'limitation' of the limitless reality of God's 'character' and presence).

You question whether my comments about Jewish teaching really reflect the opinions of Orthodox rabbis today as well as those thousands of years ago, and also ask whether or not the Law is unchanging. These questions make me realise that I need to provide a little more explanation of Judaism's understanding of the process of divine revelation.

I mentioned in an earlier letter that traditional Judaism teaches that not only were the Five Books of Moses revealed at Sinai (and not just the Ten Commandments) but also an Oral Tradition (the Oral Torah) that explained and elaborated upon the rather terse shorthand of the Written Torah. However, Judaism teaches that the revelation of God's Word and Will does not end there. The very process of applying these teachings and principles to new situations and changing conditions is seen as the working of the Holy Spirit. Thus the ongoing work of rabbinic scholarship that continues today in providing response to contemporary questions and challenges is seen as part of this corpus itself. This process is impacted upon by what may be called revelation through history. An example of this is the institution of slavery, which the Torah allows for but which became defunct both as a result of social conditions, but above all through the growing awareness on the part of the rabbis of the undesirability of the institution (in light of key biblical values, e.g. the inalienable dignity of every human person) and their reading of this attitude in the text itself (although it is by no means explicit).

However, this process leads to differences of opinion. Indeed, the Talmud is replete with disagreements between rabbis on matters of interpretation and decisions. The general resolution of these differences is through the process of scholars trying to convince one another on the basis of sacred text and tradition, eventually reaching a democratic majority opinion. Another factor, generally (but not always) determined by the former, is the position that the community of the faithful follows and which thus becomes normative practice.

Thus this democratic decision-making process among rabbinic scholars, and the interaction with the community, is itself also seen as the working of the Holy Spirit in the life of the covenanted community of Israel.

Most principles and teachings based on the sources are of course unanimously accepted. One of these is the principle that there is no atonement without *teshuvah* (repentance). On this all the rabbis are unanimous. Thus according to all rabbinic opinion an atoning sacrifice that an individual offered in the Temple was only of value as an external manifestation of an internal condition.

However, you are indeed correct in implying that the question of the restitution of the sacrificial order is a matter of debate among rabbis and scholars, with many of them believing, as you indicate, that when the Temple is rebuilt there will be a need for both. (This is probably the view of most Orthodox Jews today. However, they still do not see the Temple offerings as vicarious atonement, but simply as additional acts of devotion.)

You are correct that, in quoting Maimonides and Abrabanel, I was selecting the opinions which I share (though please note that I also quoted Midrashic, Mishnaic and prophetic sources in support as well).

Actually, your reference to Maimonides is interesting. In his Code (*Yad HaChazakah*) he refers extensively to the sacrificial order, but in his philosophical work *The Guide to the Perplexed*, he portrays it as a transitory step. This, however, is no contradiction, as in the Code he summarises all matters of Jewish practice, including the order of service in the Temple; whereas in his *Guide to the Perplexed* he offered his own opinions.

You misunderstand me when you state that I imply that the sacrificial system was a mistake, and certainly none of the rabbis whom I quote would have suggested that. Rather, the idea is that it was appropriate for the time but not an ideal for the future. As I have mentioned, there are many aspects of legislation in the Torah that take into account human needs and failures.

To take the Torah literally is indeed incompatible with normative Judaism. This was largely the orientation of the Sadducees and especially of the Karaites, who as a result cut themselves off from the Jewish mainstream. Judaism requires us to understand the written text through the prism of the Oral Tradition and exposition. Thus, for example, Judaism does not understand 'an eye for an eye and a tooth for a tooth', etc. (Exod. 21:24) in a literal sense, but rather to mean the affirmation of a principle of fair and commensurate compensation. Or another example is the prohibition against going out of one's place on the Sabbath (Exod. 16:29). Judaism does not understand this literally, but rather to mean that one should not travel away from one's home and community, etc.

So yes, you could say that I consider taking the Torah totally literally as incompatible with Judaism, as the theological postulates of Christianity are incompatible with Judaism. Your term 'intellectual suicide' sounds strange to me. I would simply say that one cannot in integrity claim to be a religious Jew and a believing Christian at the same time.

Returning again to Isaiah 52–3, I do not deny that there are those Jewish scholars who saw and may even see the text as messianic. I personally, however, concur with the majority of rabbinic opinion which does not see it as such. Of course, seeing biblical texts as containing messianic allusions is for us quite unrelated to the claims of Christians that Jesus of Nazareth is the person being alluded to. As I believe I have also stated in the past, what is important for Judaism is what happens in the Messianic Age far more than the identity of the messianic personality. Indeed, some of the prophets only talk of the

Messianic Age and not at all of a messianic personality.

However, the predominant view is that when the Almighty ushers in the era of full redemption for Israel and universal peace for humankind, He will provide a wise leader from the royal house of David who will serve as a political and spiritual guide for the Jewish people and all humanity. For this Orthodox Jews pray daily, and the concluding statement of Maimonides' Thirteen Principles of Faith in most Jewish prayer books at the conclusion of the morning service declares, 'I believe with perfect faith in the coming of the Messiah and even though he may tarry nevertheless I shall await his coming every day.'

I have a sense, RT, that the essence of our debate and discussion has now been substantially covered, although we could go on indefinitely on almost every point. I want, therefore, to conclude with some comments on how I would like us to view one another and how I believe Christianity might best be viewed from a religious Jewish perspective.

As I have indicated previously, for the majority of history most Jews have viewed Christianity and the Church's behaviour in a very negative light as a result of the disparaging and violent attitude that the Jewish community experienced in the name of Christianity and by people who called themselves Christians.

Nevertheless, there have been those who have been able to view Christianity as containing the moral values of biblical revelation and bringing these to humanity (e.g. Yehudah Halevi and Maimonides). Rabbi Menachem Meiri of Perpignan described Christians (and Muslims) as peoples bound by the ways of true religion – i.e. people who seek to live a religious moral life. Scholars like Rabbi Moses Rivkes in the seventeenth century affirmed the unique relationship between Christianity and Judaism, long before modern Jewish philosophers like Franz Rosenzweig and Martin Buber. The latter's comment that 'we share a book and a hope' were more than anticipated by Rivkes when he declared that Jews and Christians are bound together by the Hebrew Bible and its message of salvation, revelation and full messianic expectation. But arguably the boldest of all these pre-modern Orthodox rabbinic theologians was the great Rabbi Jacob Emden at the turn of the eighteenth century, who described Christianity with the Mishnaic designation as a '*knessiyah leshem shamayim shesofa lehitkayam*', i.e. 'a gathering for the sake of Heaven, of lasting validity'. (Actually the Hebrew word *knessiah*, which means gathering, is also the Hebrew word for 'church' – so it is legitimate to say that Emden is referring to Christianity as a church for the sake of Heaven that is part of divine purpose for humanity at large!)

These Jewish viewpoints see Christianity as the vehicle which through the person of Jesus of Nazareth brings God's revelation, revealed to the Jewish people through the Torah, in a more universal way to the world at large.

As a result we might be able to see ourselves as two parts of one message, each with its own integrity. One might speak of Judaism and Christianity as two different models. The one already defined community of the children of Abraham, Isaac and Jacob infused with the Divine Presence in its life and history and called to live accordingly as a light unto the nations; and the other a model by which every individual outside the former community can encounter the truths and beauty within the Sinaitic revelation. Each has its own validity, power and even complementarity for the other.

The far-reaching changes in Jewish–Christian relations during the last fifty years have led to new theological reflections in this regard. Such efforts at understanding our complementarity have included seeing Judaism and Christianity in a parallel role in which the Jewish focus on the communal Covenant with God and the Christian focus on the individual relationship with God may serve to balance one another. Others have seen the complementary relationship in that Christians need the Jewish reminder that the Kingdom of Heaven has not yet fully arrived, while Jews may benefit from the Christian awareness that in some ways that kingdom has already rooted itself in the here and now. Another view of the mutual complementarity portrays Judaism as a constant admonition to Christianity regarding the dangers of triumphalism, while Christianity's universalistic character may serve an essential role for Judaism in warning against degeneration into insular isolationism. As opposed to the underlying assumptions of the latter, there is a contention that it is actually Christianity's universalism that jars with a culturally pluralistic reality in the modern world. The communal autonomy that Judaism affirms, it is suggested, may serve more appropriately as a model for a multicultural society, while Christianity may provide a better response for individual alienation in the modern world.

These perspectives open up new ways in which Jews and Christians might be able to illumine one another while maintaining their own integrity and respect for one another.

In conclusion I would like to reiterate the importance and great potential of shared text study (which, of course, in Judaism is a sacred endeavour – even more than prayer!). While our respective different exegeses contain theological positions that are irreconcilable and make us the different faith traditions that we are, precisely because they are based upon the shared text of the Hebrew Bible we are able, if we choose, not only to enjoy the illumination of the other's tradition, but also to plumb the unlimited richness of the Hebrew Scriptures themselves, out of a shared religious commitment to them.

In this regard let me quote, in full, the statement of Martin Buber to which I referred earlier in passing:

We have in common a book and an expectation. To you the book is a forecourt; to us it is the sanctuary. But in this place we can dwell together and together listen to the voice that speaks here. That means that together we can strive to evoke the buried speech of that voice; together we can redeem the imprisoned living word.

I pray, RT, that we may be worthy of this challenge and that it might be possible for our communities to work together in genuine mutual respect to bring about that day when 'the earth will be full of the knowledge of the LORD as the waters that cover the sea' (Isa. 11:9).

Yours
David

Letter 14

Dear David

In June 2002 I addressed a group of British Christians at the Dormitian Abbey in Jerusalem, which as you know is located on Mount Zion. Some 250 of us were there on a 'Pray for the Peace of Israel' tour. A number of people from the area, including some Jewish people, had come to the Abbey for the occasion – not to hear me but to listen to London's All Souls Orchestra and Choir led by Neil Tredinik. I was asked to address the people for twenty minutes towards the end of the concert.

In my address I stated that in my opinion permanent peace will not ultimately come to Israel until the Jewish people acknowledge Jesus as their own Messiah. I predicted that lasting peace will be delayed until this happens. This is not to say we should not try every avenue available in the meantime – as you yourself have been doing for years, not to mention Canon Andrew White, who has laboured tirelessly and courageously; and as I myself in a small way have sought to do – to achieve peace in Israel. But because (1) the land of Israel is different from any other on the planet and (2) the people that reside there happen to be God's Covenant people, the normal way of making peace in the world that may have worked with other nations will not work in Israel. The God of Israel is the God of the universe and he directs the affairs of humankind. The nations to him are like 'a drop in a bucket; they are regarded as dust on the scales; he weighs the islands as though they were fine dust' (Isa. 40:15), and 'unless the LORD builds the house, its builders labour in vain. Unless the LORD watches over the city, the watchmen stand guard in vain' (Ps. 127:1). The issue, as I see it, is not political but theological.

In my talk I also asked the question, 'What if you had five minutes to address the people of Israel, what would you say?' I have thought a good deal about this, especially since meeting you, asking myself what I might choose to say if I had the opportunity to speak to every Jewish person – one at a time – or to address the whole nation at once, having to make every second count. What would I say? Having had this valuable correspondence with you, having learned so much, I will have to rethink what I might actually say if I were fortunate enough to have this privilege one day. But here are two things I said: (1) All Jews should *take another look* at *Isaiah 53 and Psalm 110*, and quoted the relevant verses that you and I have discussed in this debate together – and said what I thought such verses meant; (2) I emphasised that the *Jewish people must not forget their true identity* – that they are indeed special, the living remnant of God's ancient Covenant people. I fear that most Jewish people have forgotten their true identity, that they don't seem to realise how blessed they are to be who they are! And I then asked, by the way, who are the real friends of Israel today – are they not evangelical, Bible-believing *Christians*? Why would some people in Holland like the Corrie ten Booms and others of this world risk their lives in World War II as they did? Because they believed from the Scriptures that God's Jewish people should be protected!

I closed the address by hoping that the day will come, having based my remarks on Romans 11 and believing with all my heart that so many Israeli Jews will come to receive Jesus as their own Messiah, that they will one day say to Palestinians, 'Is it the Temple Mount you want? Take it, you can have it, we have found the reason Jesus died on the Cross 2,000 years ago and why the veil of the Temple was torn asunder from top to bottom.' And I went on to say – even if it is a pipe dream – that Palestinians would in turn say to Jewish people, 'We never thought we would ever hear you talk like that – we want what *you* have.' And then, but only then, would there be true peace in Jerusalem.

I believe that, David, to this very day.

But I must apologise one more time in behalf of thoughtless Christians over the years who have been either insensitive or incognisant of how much you and your people have suffered. You are extraordinarily gracious, absolutely magnificent – and vulnerable – to have this dialogue with me. I personally doubt there is another like you. And yet I know it is because your heart is for peace in Israel and you see this as one more way to try to make things better. And it is my fervent prayer that our debate will somehow make things better. I can assure you that Christians who read our correspondence will learn a lot, will be all the better for it, because they will now have hearts and minds illuminated with new insights and perspectives. Who knows, David, how God might use our friendship?

But when I think that so much anti-Semitism was perpetrated by certain people called Christians, I am horrified. So I am aware that we as a Church have failed you, and I am so sorry. My heart aches. If I could take a page from Nehemiah, who confessed the sins of his own generation as well as generations before him, and offer you and your people once again our apologies and sorrow over the way the Church that bears the name of Jesus has hurt you, I do so now, David.

The problem is, notwithstanding Jewish attitudes towards

what you understandably call 'a proselytising approach', the ultimate issue at the end of the day is *truth*. We who want to be obedient to our Lord bear the stigma of the claim that Jesus is not only the way but even the *truth* (John 14:6). I don't blame anybody for saying 'get off our backs' – I fully understand this. But our experience also shows that by lots of prayer and loving persistence, there have been those Jews who lived long enough to thank us for sharing the truth with them. You as a people suffer for just being *Jews*, but we who hold up the name of Jesus have suffered for the *offence of the Cross* at the hands of people of *all* ethnic backgrounds, and it was not our idea that God chose to send his one and only Son into the world to die for our sins. No human being would ever have conceived such an idea. Only the God of the Bible would have thought of this. And had the Law not preceded Jesus' coming into the world, the Cross would not have made sense. But his followers, through the illumination of the Holy Spirit, saw for themselves that the Law and the sacrificial system were pointing to what happened on that historic Good Friday in Jerusalem. This is but one reason we are eternally indebted to our Jewish roots.

Our correspondence was born in what I think was your wish to make Pharisees today look better to Christians and to those who read the New Testament. I can assure you, David, you have argued your case well. You have won that battle with ease. Christians everywhere will be deeply moved, as I have been, over your spirit, humility and kindness. I was touched by you when we first met, and I respect you even more now than I did then. Moreover, you are *not* like those men depicted in the New Testament known as Pharisees – you are too self-effacing for one thing! I have no idea what your own people will think of all this. No doubt some will criticise you, but I would have thought that a great many will salute you. I know that Christians will, as I do.

There is in my opinion one thread that possibly links you to the ancient Pharisees described in the four Gospels. This I referred to in an earlier letter to you: namely, the place those Pharisees gave to tradition. I am surmising, David, that there was inherent in ancient Pharisaism an assumed right to let time and circumstances change the authority of the written Word. You call it Oral Tradition. This is one of the things Jesus was critical of – that the Pharisees 'nullified' the Word of God by their tradition (Matt. 15:6). It seems to me that Rabbinic Judaism has allowed Oral Tradition to have priority over the Torah itself. I do not know (if this is what you are saying) that Moses gave tacit approval to Oral Tradition, or an Oral Torah, but it is fairly obvious that such has not only been made equal to the Written Torah but has even superseded Scripture. I therefore fear that my quoting any Scripture, whether from Moses or the prophets, does not carry sufficient weight with you at the end of the day.

I would welcome a continuing debate to explore the application of 'an eye for an eye' or the way slavery relates to the New Testament as well (cf. Col. 3:22ff). I am resisting the temptation to discuss what you call an 'impiety', namely, that there could be one exclusive path to God in the light of the 'limitless reality' of God's character, especially in an age of pluralism, but I suspect that you feel this too will not lead us very far. An even greater temptation for me is to pick up on what you say is the majority opinion of most orthodox Jewish rabbis today, that the Temple offerings would be seen not as vicarious atonement but as 'additional acts of devotion'. Most of all, I would have wanted to discuss what seems to be the case, that the messianic hope of modern Israel is largely anticipating an *age*, not a person – as used to be the case.

The truth is, is it not, David, that normative Judaism at some stage crossed over an epistemological line – from a robust doctrine of revelation to a different way of knowing. Therefore the application of the Hebrew Scriptures today becomes that which the majority – what you call 'the working of the Holy Spirit' – decides to be true. If I have misunderstood you I hope you will extend the correspondence since this is crucial in our mutual interchange. But if I have generally assessed things correctly, I acknowledge that I was not prepared for this when our correspondence commenced. It has not in the slightest changed my enthusiasm to dialogue with you. I am only saying that I have had to make a major adjustment in my perception of what I thought you believed as an Orthodox Jewish rabbi. But you, David, are being true to yourself, as Shakespeare said one must do, and I respect you for this.

I therefore concur that the essence of our debate and discussion has now been substantially covered, and I am prepared to bring the 'public' part of our debate to a halt. I do hope you will allow me to correspond with you on and on and have more Shabbat meals together.

I feel I must say three things before I conclude. First, I want to leave you with my personal testimony. You may secretly wonder why I *really* – in my heart of hearts – hold to the vicarious atonement of Jesus for the sins of the world on Good Friday and his literal resurrection from the dead on the third day. It is because of two things – apart from my belief in Holy Scripture: (1) the immediate witness of the Holy Spirit; and (2) the effect my faith has had on my personal life.

Many years ago, as I drove in my car in Tennessee, I was carried up to what might be called 'the third heaven' (2 Cor. 12:2). The person of Jesus was more real to me than anyone or anything around me. I saw him. He was real – a real human being and interceding for me at the right hand of God. I was overjoyed. The peace that was given me was the most wonderful experience of my life. I knew that Jesus was truly raised from the dead, that he was coming again and that I myself was eternally saved. My own theology was utterly renovated. This experience, David, is what held me when later on I faced the challenge of pluralism, neo-Orthodoxy, biblical criticism, process theology and existentialism. I credit my faith to the sheer grace of God, and to his kindness in granting me the gift of the Holy Spirit that made all I believe so real that I would stake my life on it, even if I had to stand utterly alone against the world.

It is my view that the gift of the Holy Spirit was one of the main reasons 3,000 Jews asked for baptism on the day of Pentecost (Acts 2:41). It is not that they questioned the content of Peter's sermon, for they obviously believed every word of it. But what gripped them was *what had actually just happened* to those 120 souls on whom the Holy Spirit fell: their speaking in unknown languages, hearing what was said in one's own language, the phenomena of the wind and the fire, and, possibly most of all, the conduct of the 120 that made people think they were drunk on new wine (Acts 2:4–13)! I doubt people would have mocked these 120 men and women over the supernatural phenomena that they witnessed, but I reckon that the 120 were so filled with joy and laughter that they gave observers reason to think they must be drunk! Whatever it was, it was what 3,000 wanted for themselves because Peter had to say to them that they, too, could receive the gift of the Spirit if they repented and were baptised (Acts 2:38).

I have given a lot of thought (and speculation) as to what might lift or remove the main obstacles which make it difficult for Jews to recognise Jesus – *Yeshua* – as their Messiah. I wonder if the biggest obstacle may have been the Church and the attitudes and demeanour of Christians. I fear that we do not manifest this same joy as I just described, but are so guilty of pointing the finger all the time at those who disagree with us. If this assessment is correct, it is shameful. But on the other hand I have wondered if the conversion of Palestinians could make a difference. One of my reasons for doing all I could to convince the late Yasser Arafat to accept Jesus was precisely this. It was partly based on Romans 11. Since the conversion of Gentiles was seen as possibly provoking Israel to 'envy' (Rom. 11:11, 14), it crossed my mind more than once that his coming to faith in Jesus could make a difference among Israeli Jews. Or I wonder if what would make it easy for Jewish people to accept Jesus as their Messiah could be the restoration of signs and wonders to the Church, something I personally pray for every day. I am sure in any case it will not bypass God's ordained means, namely, the proclamation of the Word (1 Cor. 1:21). It will have to be a sovereign work of the Holy Spirit. But I think, too, the fulfilment of Romans 11:24 ('how much more readily will these, the natural branches, be grafted into their own olive tree!') may be when we Christians show such a change in our lives that we will make people *want* what we have. We see too little of this, David. I am guilty as anyone, and I cannot defend it. I am just sorry.

That brings me to the second thing, the change my faith has made in my own life. When I came across the teaching of total forgiveness (the title of one of my books), it literally saved my life and ministry. I went through such trials, both in my church and in my marriage, that had I not discovered first-hand the joy of the Holy Spirit that comes from *totally forgiving* everybody in the world, living or dead, who had hurt me or carried out some injustice, I would not have survived. The teaching of total forgiveness comes right out of the life of Joseph (the way he forgave his brothers – Genesis 45) and became the heart of Jesus' teaching. Once I took this seriously, I was changed all over again as a person as much as the aforementioned experi-ence changed me when driving in my car. Experiencing *total forgiveness* from God and towards others made me a better husband, a better father and a better Christian. This is why I know that what I believe is true: it works.

And yet I too often forget this in my witnessing for the Lord, and resort to cerebral arguments as if such will make the world come running to Jesus. I am reminded of a poem my wife Louise brought to my attention:

> For me 'twas not the truth you taught,
> To you so clear, to me so dim;
> But when you came to me, you brought
> A sense of Him.
>
> And from your eyes He beckons me,
> And from your heart His love is shed,
> Till I lose sight of you and see
> The Christ instead.
>
> Beatrice Clelland

The third and final word, as I bring my last letter to you to a close, is to quote my friend Joni Eareckson Tada, a legendary woman in America whose accident when swimming as a teenager left her quadriplegic: 'I am a Christian not because of what Christianity does for me but because it's true.' This is all that ultimately matters. It is a *fact* that Jesus was crucified outside the city of Jerusalem 2,000 years ago, and those who believed in his resurrection from the dead did so because it was a *fact*, not something they made up.

Thank you for providing a theological framework for continuing dialogue between Christians and Jews. I can see this has been carefully thought out and I see further why you are so wonderfully used in this area all over the world. I would love to know whether you envisage that one with my own views (you know me pretty well by now!) could fit in with this. I will do all within my power to keep doors open to Jews, Muslims and all Christians with whom I might have some disagreement; for I am no isolationist. I suppose I just need to know from you that a person with my views is welcome in any peace or reconciliation process.

So, David, I appeal to your graciousness one more time and ask you and all Jewish people to forgive us Christians for entering so often where angels fear to tread without the love and joy of the Holy Spirit. Thank you for the inestimable privilege of having this correspondence with you. I have enjoyed every minute of it. Please know that I thank God with all my heart for your friendship.

The LORD bless you and keep you; the LORD make his face shine upon you and be gracious to you; the LORD turn his face toward you and give you peace.

(Num. 6:24–6)

Your friend
RT

Conclusion

It is a reflection of the magnanimity of R.T. Kendall that he has graciously insisted that I have the last word in this book.

We have shared what evidently has been enjoyable discussion for us both, and when enquiring about each other's beliefs, practices and interpretations of Scripture, I believe that it has been an edifying experience. I am sure that I speak for RT as well when I express the hope that the reader will also be able to both benefit from and enjoy this exchange.

However, at the heart of this debate there is an unbridgeable chasm, which is a Christian conviction not only that Christianity is the possessor of absolute and exclusive truth but that its interpretation of Scripture is the only true understanding possible.

R.T. Kendall makes an interesting point (in fact an accusation) in his final letter which I cannot dismiss. While he has acknowledged my point that the Pharisees as a general group have received a 'bad rap' (which does not mean that baskets of good fruit do not often contain rotten apples here and there), he suggests that there is 'one thread that possibly links [me] to the ancient Pharisees described in the four Gospels' and that is 'the place these Pharisees gave to tradition' to the degree that 'not only [has it] been made equal to the Written Torah but has even superseded it'.

Obviously Christians, like anyone else, may view rabbinic Jewish emphasis upon the importance of the Oral Tradition as they choose. But it is essential for me to clarify that we do not see this emphasis as 'nullifying' the Written Torah but rather as explaining it. As I mentioned in one of my letters, there is so much of the Pentateuch that simply *cannot* be understood without commentary. The example I gave was of the commandment to keep the Sabbath holy (Exod. 19:8 and Deut. 5:12). What does that mean? How do you do that? Another example would be the commandment to dwell in booths on the Festival of Tabernacles (Lev. 23:42). What is a booth? How do you make one? Furthermore, which is the fruit of a goodly tree, and what is a branch of the thick tree that one is meant to take with a palm frond and willows on that festival (Lev. 23:40)? Indeed, what does 'take' mean and what is it for? One could go on and on. But what I wish to clarify here is that it is actually impossible to understand the whole Bible literally. As a result, Judaism does indeed give unique weight to the Oral Tradition, but precisely because it believes that the Written Tradition can only be *accessed* through the former. Moreover, because Judaism is a living tradition, it is continuously relating to changing conditions.

For those who believe that it is possible and correct to read the Bible literally, this must indeed be a perplexing if not an irritating thing.

However, I might repeat here a point I make in one of my letters, that this was actually the criticism of the Sadducees (who rejected the Oral Tradition) against the Pharisees. Ironically, the Sadducees were actually the religious and political Jewish establishment at the time of Jesus, who apparently handed him over to the Roman authorities with whom they collaborated. This literalist approach was also the attitude of the Karaites a number of centuries later. They were/are a group that broke away from Rabbinic Judaism, and some Karaite communities still remain in different parts of the world, including Israel, albeit in tiny numbers (a few thousand), as a sect quite separate from Jewry.

R. T. Kendall suggests that 'at the end of the day' the reason why his 'quoting any Scriptures, whether from Moses or the prophets, does not carry sufficient weight with [me]' is because I don't take the text seriously enough. But I would claim the contrary and suggest that the reason I don't accept his claims is that without a Christian experience there is absolutely no objective basis for Christian faith claims in the texts he quotes. In fact, Christianity itself makes an 'oral tradition' the key to understanding Scripture. That 'oral tradition' is the faith in Jesus and Christians' own experience of it, and it is accordingly that faith which is used to reinterpret the texts as referring to that which Christianity believes them to allude to.

The fact is that Rabbinic Judaism and Christianity are both interpretations of the Hebrew biblical text. We share that text but differ on our interpretations of it. I would like us to be able to recognise that and respect it. I would even like us to consider the possibility that there actually may be divine purpose and intention in the very existence of our different (but I would say, parallel) paths to the One Truth. I believe that such perception could be mutually enriching and enlightening.

So aside from my desire to educate non-Jews about Judaism and combat misrepresentations and possible prejudice, my interest in seeing this correspondence published is also a reflection of my commitment to Jewish–Christian dialogue.

While I would like the whole world to acknowledge the One Lord Creator and Guide of the Universe (in keeping with the vision of Zechariah 14:9, 'in that day He shall be One and the Name shall be One') and above all to observe His way (Gen. 18:19) of justice, righteousness and loving kindness,

Judaism does not aspire to make everyone Jewish. While we are charged to accept those who wish to convert to Judaism with special love, Judaism insists that the 'righteous of the nations have their portion in the world to come'. There is no need to be Jewish in order to 'get one's ticket through the pearly gates'! In other words, there is more than one path to Heaven.

Moreover, I believe that the encounter with wisdom and insight from different traditions is an enriching and ennobling experience.

However, the relationship between Judaism and Christianity is unique, for we each see ourselves as rooted in the history of the divine message revealed in the Hebrew Bible. I quoted Martin Buber's comment that Christians and Jews 'share a book and a hope'. But the paradox is that that book which unites us often divides us, because we have come to interpret its meaning and terms in different ways.

This does not at all have to be an obstacle to mutual understanding, respect and even enrichment. But it does require us, if we are to dialogue honestly, to recognise this fact and to be informed about those differing interpretations and under-standings.

Buber also refers to a 'hope'. Similarly, that messianic expect-ation that we share also divides us. But surely, even if we are divided in its interpretation to a substantial degree, there is still much that we can and must do in practice to bring about the kingdom of Heaven on earth. And surely if there are moral, ethical and social values that we do share, we have an obligation to them as well as to their Source, to work together for their realisation with all who affirm them!

The 'book' also links us to the land of Israel. Of course, the relationship of Christianity to the Holy Land is not the same as it is for Judaism, which sees it not just as a national homeland but the place – as stated in the Bible – where the children of

Israel should ideally live the way of life revealed to them at Sinai. Nevertheless, by virtue of the special link of the Jewish people with the land, it became the birthplace of Christianity, contains venerable Christian communities within it and is a place of pilgrimage for Christians from around the world.

All this surely places an additional common responsibility upon us to promote the well-being of all who live in this land, Jews, Christians and Muslims.

Inevitably the conflict in the Middle East elicits very partisan views, and there are Christians whose unqualified support for the state of Israel (often out of a belief that Israel is the vehicle by which the Second Coming, Armageddon and the universal triumph of Christianity will arrive) leads them to disregard the needs, well-being and aspirations of Palestinians. There are other Christians whose identification with Palestinians, whether through their own links with Arab Christians or simply out of empathy for the Palestinian plight, leads them to insensitivity and even hostility towards Israel's needs and well-being.

Accordingly, I am so grateful for the work of those Christians who genuinely care for all who live in this land and who through prayer or action or both seek to contribute to reconciliation and peace.

This was how I met R. T. Kendall, through my involvement with and his support of the Alexandria process. The Alexandria summit initiated by Lord George Carey, then Archbishop of Canterbury, and directed by his emissary Canon Andrew White, brought leaders and representatives of the religious establishments in the Holy Land together for the first time ever in history. That fact is both pathetic and wonderful. Pathetic that it had never happened before – and wonderful that it actually took place.

I presume to believe that the fact that this initiative was led by Christians was not coincidental. Indeed, Christians have very much been the pioneers of interreligious dialogue in the

Holy Land over recent decades, but this has generally been marginal and has not impacted upon the religious institutions and their leadership. There is now a remarkable change in this regard, and I think that Christians of genuine goodwill to both peoples in the Holy Land can play a special role in promoting understanding, cooperation and peace, if these efforts are done in a manner that respects the particular identities, faith affirmations and attachments involved.

This is not an easy matter for those who believe that everyone should share their own faith affirmations. However, few things will undermine sincere Christian efforts to help bring peace in the Middle East more than the perception on the part of Jews and Muslims that the reason for such initiatives is simply to advance an exclusive Christian theological agenda. So those like RT who have the passionate burning need to persuade others of their conviction, and who wish to be peacemakers at the same time, have to decide which of these roles will get the better of the other.

Another testimony of RT's magnanimity was his declared desire that anyone reading our exchange would be impressed by both of our arguments. Nevertheless, our hopes remain rather different. I hope that Christians reading this book will remain Christians, just as I hope Jews will remain Jews. However, I do also hope that readers will be impressed by the fact that, notwithstanding our profound differences, it is possible to discuss even these respectfully without pulling any punches; that it is possible to say and hear tough things and still remain (indeed, even grow as) loving friends. In that in itself there is surely testimony to the Divine Presence, compassion and love in our midst, and for this I express my thanks and affection to R.T. Kendall for having initiated this endeavour. May it be a source of blessing and enlightenment.

Rabbi David Rosen

Appendix

The sin Jesus hated most

(from Chapter 7 of R.T. Kendall's book *Out of the Comfort Zone*, Hodder & Stoughton, 2005)

In the four Gospels, the Pharisees are almost entirely portrayed as the bad guys. And yet I keep in mind that on at least one occasion Jesus accepted an invitation to have dinner with a Pharisee (Luke 11:37). The meal was paralleled by Jesus ruthlessly exposing the hearts of the Pharisees – who he tended to put altogether in one lump – and called them 'You foolish people' (v. 40). The Pharisee might have been a nice man, but Jesus was not very nice to him!

The Pharisees (a word which probably means the 'separated ones') emerged in the second century BC. They were a strict sect made up mostly of ordinary Jews, unlike the Sadducees who were members of the families of priests. Pharisees were far more numerous than Sadducees but not so prestigious. The Pharisees kept closely to the Mosaic Law and often embellished the Law with countless rules so that these rules were very hard to keep. They saw themselves as a cut above everybody else. They counted work on the Sabbath as walking more than a kilometre from one's town, carrying any kind of load or lighting a fire in the home. It led to people being concerned to keep the Law in every detail. The Pharisees believed that their rules built a 'fence around the Law' so that by keeping these rules people would be in less danger of disobeying the actual Law of God.

One must not forget that many of them were no doubt pious men. Some scholars reckon that when Jesus described the Pharisee in the parable in Luke 18:9–14, some Pharisees really did do such things as he boasted of – fasting twice a week and giving a tenth of all they earned, not to mention the fact that they would never be guilty of wrongdoing such as robbing or committing adultery. They were regarded as the truly righteous people of their day. They were without question the backbone of their synagogues and would in some cases be like certain evangelicals today who carry their big black Bibles to church and would never smoke or touch a drop of alcohol or watch a movie that was anything but for the whole family. But they tended to look down on those who did not keep their rules and called such people 'sinners'. Remember too that Nicodemus, who was a secret follower of Jesus, was a Pharisee. So was the apostle Paul before he was converted.

But given the fact that Pharisees were pious, faithful and the stalwarts of the synagogues in ancient Judaism, why was Jesus so hard on them? Should he not have congratulated them, as if to say, 'You are greatly needed here in Jerusalem these days. I can't imagine what things would be like were it not for you.' No. He never congratulated them once or gave the slightest hint they were either needed or appreciated. He was harsh and rugged with them.

What is most interesting to me is that Jesus was patient,

loving and gracious to the woman caught in the sin of adultery, unlike the Pharisees who were chuffed (but supposedly indignant) that they found this woman in the act of sin (John 8:1–11). Jesus did not ever appear to show tender feelings towards the Pharisees. He was not very nice to them, despite the fact that they upheld the infallibility of the Bible, believed in resurrected life beyond the grave (unlike the Sadducees) and adhered to a number of practices which Jesus also affirmed.

When I was a young Christian I used to wonder why so much attention was given in the four Gospels to the Pharisees since they do not exist today. Was this not a waste of space? Why should we have to read about irrelevant people? I have since learned, of course, that Pharisees do indeed exist today.

The Pharisees' comfort zone

Their traditions

Their extra-biblical rules became a tradition that you were required to keep or you did not love God or respect the Law. Some Pharisees came up to Galilee all the way from Jerusalem just to ask Jesus, 'Why do your disciples break the tradition of the elders? They don't wash their hands before they eat!' (Matt. 15:1–2). Imagine being so threatened by Jesus that one walks for three days just to see why he did not keep certain rules! This washing of hands was not merely a health matter, by the way, it was a ritualistic thing you did that showed you adhered to the 'party line'.

How they found significance

One thing in particular was, according to Jesus, that they sought to achieve significance in being admired. 'They loved to be greeted in the market-places and to have men call them "Rabbi"' (Matt. 23:7). They 'loved the praise from men more

than praise from God' (John 12:43). That was the essence of
their comfort zone: being applauded, being complimented,
being respected and being openly referred to. Do that and you
had no problem with them. Jesus didn't do that and had
problems with them. These pious men were right in the middle
of the conspiracy to have Jesus crucified (John 11:45–7).

They further sought significance like this: they compared
themselves with others – always people they could safely label
'sinners'. That way they always came out on top. So in the
aforementioned parable the Pharisee boasted of his good works,
then added: 'God, I thank you that I am not like other men –
robbers, evildoers, adulterers – or even like this tax collector'
(Luke 18:11). We can all find someone who is less righteous
than we are to whom we can compare ourselves and we
therefore come forth smelling like a rose. 'Comparisons are
odious,' said Shakespeare, referring to comparing one person
against another; but it is perhaps even more odious when we
do this to make ourselves look good. 'At least I'm not as bad as
so–and–so.'

They even got their sense of significance in the way they
dressed. 'Oh yes,' said Jesus. 'Everything they do is done for
men to see: They make their phylacteries wide and the tassels
on their garments long' (Matt. 23:5). Dress is very important
to a Pharisee; always has been, always will be. They will not be
the slightest bit convicted over holding a grudge or speaking
evil of fellow believers, but they go to pains to look good.

We are talking about the chief enemies of Jesus – who saw
right through them – who found their significance in what
people said positively about them, by comparing themselves
with others and by their very appearance. I wonder how many
preachers today need the good suit or clerical garb just to look
successful in order to feel important and significant. If I am not
careful I will end up a Pharisee in judging them, but I only
know so many give the impression, even if unintentionally,

that their appearance is an essential ingredient to their sense of significance.

Motivation

How do you persuade a Pharisee to give to the poor? The answer is very simple: hire a couple of trumpeters – a band would be better – and get everyone's attention with the music. They announced their giving by the sound of trumpets in the synagogues and on the streets for one reason: 'to be seen of men'. And how do you suppose you get a Pharisee to pray? Jesus said, 'They love to pray.' If Jesus had said only that they love to pray he would have complimented them. I love to pray. Do you love to pray? Nothing wrong with loving to pray. For that's good. But with the Pharisees, 'They love to pray standing in the synagogues and on the street corners to be seen by men.' The way you get them to stop praying is to walk away while they are doing it. For there is no motivation left if no one is noticing.

And since we know that Pharisees fasted twice a week, what do you suppose lay behind that worthy practice? They made sure you saw them. First, they looked sombre (possibly not too hard for some Pharisees anyway). Second, they disfigured their faces – they put on a facial expression that told you they were carrying heavy-duty burdens; this was important stuff, mind you. They didn't even comb their hair (they were afraid you wouldn't otherwise notice) when they skipped a meal or two. Read it all in Matthew 5:1–18.

In a word: they were starving for recognition. As long as they got credit for giving, praying or fasting, you could count on them – every time. Take away the credit, the tax exemption, the plaque on the wall, the public knowledge of a generous donation, the thanks before all for doing the flowers in front of the pulpit or for washing up in the church kitchen, then there aren't many in the queue wanting to help.

The problem with Pharisees was they so often had no objectivity about themselves. This is because their main problem was that they had no sense of sin. None. Sin to them was always in what you do or don't do. Not what you think or feel. It was all outward appearance. They forgot that God looks on the heart (1 Sam. 16:7).

Priorities

The theological assumptions and priorities of Pharisees can be quickly summed up: their theology was more important than people. They really didn't care about people. It was all theology. Hold to the truth. Contend for the faith. Keep the party line. Above all, remember the Sabbath.

It is almost hilarious that Jesus again and again seemed to wait for the Sabbath before he healed people. Read Matthew 12:2, Mark 2:24, Luke 6:2 and 6, and Luke 14:3 for a start. You get the picture that he sees a needy person but says to himself, 'It's only two more days until the Sabbath is here and I will wait in order to heal this person then.' In other words, Jesus attacked the Pharisees – not for their upholding the Law but for putting their traditions and party line alongside Holy Scripture as if they were of the same authority. There isn't a single word in the Law that says a person should not be made well on the Sabbath.

This partly is why they hated all that Jesus preached and did. He did not hold to the party line. They never saw their own sin – ever, as far as we can tell. This is why Jesus said that it was the tax collector, so looked down on by the Pharisee, who was justified before God rather than the Pharisee. For the tax collector prayed, not even being able to look up to Heaven, but beat his breast and said, 'God, have mercy on me, a sinner' (Luke 18:13–14).

They further perpetuated their comfort zones by loopholes they somehow found that set them free from the kind of obedience they were uncomfortable with. The fences that they erected that supposedly protected the Law actually served in some cases to give a way out *not* to obey the Law strictly at all! Jesus nailed them to the wall in this area. The commandment to honour both father and mother was undeniable – this being the Fifth Commandment. But they had a way of keeping their parents from receiving money that ought to go to them by a rule that enabled them to divert it to the temple or synagogue instead.

> You [Pharisees] say that if a man says to his father or mother, 'Whatever help you might otherwise have received from me is a gift devoted to God [the money should go to the Lord instead in this case],' he is not to 'honour his father' with it. Thus you nullify the word of God for the sake of your tradition.
>
> (Matt. 15:5–6)

When Jesus said that one cannot enter the kingdom of Heaven unless one's righteousness actually surpasses that of the Pharisees, nobody could believe their ears. For the ordinary Jew living at the time thought they were so far beneath a Pharisee; the thought of exceeding the righteousness of a Pharisee seemed over the top. But Jesus knew exactly what he was talking about; not only are we justified by faith in Jesus who perfectly fulfilled the Law in our behalf but our very righteousness, when we follow Jesus, far outdistances that of the Pharisee. For the Pharisee never felt any conscience about speaking evil of another, hurting their reputation, holding a grudge or not forgiving an enemy.

We are getting closer to the answer to the question posed above, since Pharisees were vanguards for the Law and were moral and sound on many essential matters. Why didn't Jesus congratulate them? Why was he so hard on them? Even if he

saw through them, that they were phoney in their righteousness, why didn't he leave them alone and attack wicked tax
collectors, harlots and drunkards?

The answer is: they did so much harm. They converted
people over to their party line and made that person 'twice as
much a son of hell as you are' (Matt. 23:15). People like this get
more excited over changing a person's theology to suit their
own than they do about leading a person to Christ. They will
spend more time attacking an enemy who threatens them than
going into the world to save the lost. It is like King Saul, who
was more worried about young David than he was the arch-
enemy of Israel – the Philistines! This is how lopsided people
can get and why Jesus knew the Pharisees were dangerous.
They did harm to people.

One of the hardest things Jesus said to them was this: 'You
shut the kingdom of heaven in men's faces. You yourselves do
not enter, nor will you let those enter who are trying to' (Matt.
23:14).

But Jesus also knew that Pharisees would be the ones who
would lead the way to his own death. There was never a thought
that such a conspiracy would be instigated by the notorious
sinners of the day – drunkards, whoremongers, adulterers or
even murderers. Not that they were incapable of such. But,
generally speaking, people like that don't tend to send an
innocent man to the Cross. But religious people do. Jesus
therefore had their number and declared war on them from
almost the first time he opened his mouth. 'Do not think that
I have come to abolish the Law,' he said early on in the Sermon
on the Mount (Matt. 5:17). Why say that? Why bring that
subject up? It was because Jesus wanted to get to the heart of
the matter as soon as possible. When he began to attack their
interpretations of the Law he knew he would be in a constant
battle with them from then on. It worked. They led the way in
getting him crucified. But that is what he came to do! He

came to die on the Cross for our sins and, in the meantime, establish the kind of people who would be saved. 'I have not come to call the righteous [by which he meant those who purport to be righteous] but sinners to repentance' (Luke 5:32).

'The common people heard him gladly' (Mark 12:37, AV). On one occasion they sent a temple guard to bring Jesus in so they could arrest him. But these guards came back shortly – but without Jesus. 'Why didn't you bring him in?' they were asked.

The guards replied, 'No one ever spoke the way this man does.'

'You mean he has deceived you also?' the Pharisees retorted.

This sort of thing thrust Pharisees right out of their comfort zone. They resorted to their theology: 'this mob [people following Jesus] . . . knows nothing of the law' (John 7:45–9). Their ultimate weapon against common Jews was the threat of putting anybody out of the synagogue who confessed faith in Jesus (John 12:42). The typical ploy of a Pharisee is to motivate by fear.

Their attack lay in the idea of 'guilt by association'. This tactic was used by Pharisees then and continues to be used today. If people who are attracted to you – or people you spend time with – are unworthy, theologically inarticulate, not of good stock or of respectable credentials, all of you are in the same boat together and should be regarded as being cut out of the same cloth. You are all equally guilty. You prove your guilt by those you are friendly with.

The Pharisees' trump card therefore: the kind of people that Jesus allowed to be around him, the quality of people affirming him and the backgrounds of those who were brought closest to him. 'This man welcomes sinners, and eats with them' (Luke 15:2). This, to the Pharisees, should be enough to indict Jesus as one to be shunned and should surely cause everybody to turn against Jesus! But it didn't work. Jesus even pleaded guilty to the charge and told several more parables (Luke 15 and 16) to show that the Father loves and welcomes sinners into his family.

Pharisees yesterday and today love to repudiate a person by the quality of the people they seek to reach or who admire them. Jesus surprised everybody by choosing a tax collector to be one of the twelve disciples. That was just not on! The Pharisees on the other hand quickly write off those who mix with those who do not adhere to their party line.

The worst thing of all, however, was this. The Pharisees' search for significance outside God and from the praise of people lay at the bottom of their inability to recognise God's Messiah when he stood before their very eyes. Have you wondered why ancient Israel missed out when Messiah came? Have you wondered why they still reject him? I can tell you. It is because they chose the immediate gratification of receiving praise from people rather than to seek what it would have been like had they sought the honour that comes only from God. Seeking the honour, praise and glory that comes from God alone means letting go of the applause of men and women. It also means a lot of patience. Because you don't feel anything the first day when you make this a life-long pursuit. So it isn't easy. The Pharisees said that not only is it too hard but also they simply weren't going to go that route. Surely their reverence for the Law was good enough. The Law is God's product; the Law isn't God himself. And those who give priority to the Law inevitably end up as Pharisees and miss out on God's next move, just as the Jews missed out on their own Messiah.

Therefore Jesus was not surprised at their refusal to believe in him. He gave the explanation himself and summed up their unbelief in a simple question he asked, 'How can you [how could you possibly] believe if you accept praise from one another, yet make no effort to obtain the praise that comes from the only God?' (John 5:44). They made a choice: they preferred compliments, adoration, admiration and glory from people. Jesus said they 'made no effort' to see what it would have been like had they sought their significance in the sheer glory of God. But they opted for the glory of man. This felt better. Possibly, for a while. But at the end of the day one who makes this choice will pay for it dearly and suffer for it bitterly – forever – unless God mercifully steps down as he did in the cases of Nicodemus and Saul of Tarsus. And me. And I hope you.

What breaks your heart is that the Pharisees were the ones who led to Jesus' weeping over the city of Jerusalem, in a lengthy denunciation of the Pharisees in Matthew 23. It culminated in Jesus crying out,

> O Jerusalem, Jerusalem, you who kill the prophets and stone those sent to you, how often I have longed to gather your children together, as a hen gathers her chicks under her wings, but you were not willing. Look, your house is left to you desolate.
>
> (Matt. 22:37–8)

This is the way Chapter 7 was concluded in my book Out of the Comfort Zone – Is Your God Too Nice? *I will not repeat any of Chapter 8, partly written humorously, 'Twenty-six reasons you may be a Pharisee'. Let me remind you that Rabbi David Rosen read all of both chapters. The first letter he wrote in response to my stuff is Chapter 1 of the present book. The rest speaks for itself. It is our wish that the book will create an ever-increasing love and understanding between Christians and Jews. I myself have learned so much. Keep also in mind that, whereas the ancient Pharisees were pre-eminently concerned with what people thought, Rabbi Rosen has come forward with remarkable courage and risks his reputation by being associated with me and this book.*

Glossary

Abrabanel (or Abarbanel) – Isaac the son of Judah, fifteenth-century statesman, philosopher and biblical commentator.

Adonai – literally 'my Lord', using the most respectful grammatical construct (i.e. plural). The word is used by Jews only to denote God.

Aggadah – the non-legal or homiletical corpus of the TALMUD and MIDRASH.

Akiva – arguably the greatest Jewish sage of the period of the MISHNAH. He systematised the structure and content of the ORAL TRADITION. He was tortured to death by the Romans for his promotion of the practice and study of Judaism after these had been outlawed subsequent to the failure of the BAR COCHBA rebellion in 135 CE.

Annihilationism – the denial of conscious eternal punishment, the belief that the entire person (body, soul, spirit, mind) is rendered non-existent after death or Final Judgment, as though he or she had never been created.

Antinomianism – literally 'against law', this word was

invented by MARTIN LUTHER to refer to a teaching which denied the role of the Law in the Christian life. Although many who have been called 'antinomian' have been godly people, the word tends to be used to mean 'licentiousness'.

Anti-Semitism – the term used to denote prejudice and hostility against Jews.

Ashkenazi(c) – Jews who live in/originate from Christian (European) lands. More specifically, those who follow particular German/Polish customs and order of prayers.

Atonement – the Jewish view: the process by which a person is purified from sin through repentance and good works. The Christian view: a sacrifice which has the effect of cancelling the guilt of sin. This is achieved through Jesus' death when ratified by one's faith.

Augustine (354–430) – major Christian theologian born and raised in North Africa. Bishop of Hippo; considered a saint by the Church.

Bar Cochba (bar Coziba) – Simon, the leader of the Jewish rebellion against Rome that was initially successful in the year 132 CE. Perceived as the anticipated Messiah by the people, he was given the name Bar Cochba meaning 'Son of the Star' (in keeping with Numbers 24:17). Ultimately the rebellion was put down ruthlessly by the Romans in the year 135, leading to severe repression of the practice and study of Judaism as well as mass exile. Bar Cochba then became popularly referred to as Bar Coziba, meaning 'the Son of Falsehood (false hopes)'.

BCE – Before the Common (or Christian) era (see CE).

Billerbeck, Paul – nineteenth-century German scholar of New Testament and rabbinic literature.

Buber, Martin (1878–1965) – Jewish philosopher/theologian, born in Vienna; immigrated to Palestine (later Israel) where he taught social philosophy at the Hebrew University of Jerusalem.

Calvin, John – sixteenth-century French theologian who lived in Geneva. One of the fathers of Protestant Christianity. He was a proponent of the doctrine that salvation is obtained only by divine grace and that faith is an unconditional divine gift.

CE – the Christian Era (or the Common Era), a form of dating that many Jews prefer to AD, as the latter designates Jesus as Lord.

Ceremonial Law – those aspects of religious practice that relate to ceremonies and rituals.

Chief Rabbi – one who is appointed to a position of Jewish communal religious authority, often involving the licensing and appointments of other rabbis as well as overseeing matters of religious personal status (marriage, divorce, etc.) within a specific Jewish community. Primarily, chief rabbinates were established to fulfil a representative role to the non-Jewish authorities.

Christian – a faithful follower of Jesus who is acclaimed as the God–man and Christ (i.e. Messiah).

Circumcised – a male whose foreskin of the penis has been removed.

Civil law – the secular law of the land.

Codes – extensive guidebooks to Jewish practice and observance.

Conservative Judaism – one of the main streams of modern Judaism (Conservative and Reform Jews make up some 90 per cent of the identifying Jewish community of the USA). It emerged out of what was known in the nineteenth century as

Positive-Historical Judaism. The term 'Conservative' does not mean that the movement's adherents are politically conservative. Rather, the term denotes that Jews should 'conserve' religious tradition rather than radically reform it, let alone abandon it. However, the Conservative movement teaches that Judaism has adapted to changing conditions throughout history. Accordingly, as opposed to predominant Orthodox Jewish attitudes, the Conservative view is that Judaism can and must adapt itself to modernity and modern needs. Conservative Judaism therefore occupies a middle position between Orthodox and Reform Judaism. The Conservative movement is now overwhelmingly egalitarian, and in recent decades has introduced the ordination of women for the rabbinate.

Constantine (the Great) – born in the late third century, he was the son of a Roman officer and became emperor of Rome. After his conversion to Christianity, his empire became known as the Holy Roman Empire, in which Christianity was the state religion.

Council of Trent – the nineteenth Ecumenical council of the Catholic Church, which took place in the mid-sixteenth century with the main object of defining the doctrines of the Church in answer to the 'heresies' of the PROTESTANTS. The Council also sought to implement a thorough reform of the inner life of the Church by removing numerous abuses that had developed within it.

Covenant (including NOAHIDE COVENANT, ABRAHAMIC COVENANT and SINAI COVENANT) – the Hebrew word *brit* indicates a binding commitment between parties and is used in the Hebrew Bible to designate God's undertaking and expectations accordingly.

The Noahide Covenant (i.e. Covenant with Noah and his descendants) reflects God's commitment to care for all humanity and not destroy it (Gen. 9:9–11). In return He expects all humanity to lead a moral life (Gen. 9:4–6).

The Abrahamic Covenant contains the basic promise that Abraham will be given 'seed' (descendants) and inherit the land of his sojourning. The Christian view is that the seed refers to Jesus and to those who believe in the promise; this became the foundation of Paul's teaching of JUSTIFICATION BY FAITH (Rom. 4).

The Sinai Covenant (Exod. 19) is the confirmation of God's everlasting commitment to the children of Israel (the children of Abraham, Isaac and Jacob) and His expectation that they would live in accordance with the revelation at Mount Sinai (which according to Jewish tradition means all the commandments in the Pentateuch). The Christian view is that Jesus fulfilled the Law by his sinless life and sacrificial death, and that his followers would out of gratitude uphold the righteousness of the Law.

Day of Atonement – the tenth day of the Hebrew month of Tishrei, when it is prohibited to eat or drink (for twenty-five hours). The day of fasting and prayer is devoted to seeking divine forgiveness for sins in keeping with Leviticus 23:27–32 (see also Lev. 16).

Decalogue – literally 'the Ten Sayings', commonly known as the Ten Commandments.

Deity – God.

Divine Presence – in Hebrew *Shekhinah*, indicating God's indwelling in a specific place or in the world at large.

Elect – chosen.

Eschatology – the theology of the end of days.

Essenes – a semi-monastic Jewish sect that functioned in the late Second Temple period and is generally associated with the Qumran community on the west shore of the Dead Sea.

Evangelicals – PROTESTANT Christians who uphold the divine inspiration of Scripture, the TRINITY and the essential teachings of the NEW TESTAMENT such as the need for all people to be saved through the vicarious ATONEMENT of Jesus Christ and his bodily resurrection. They also believe in his Second Coming and the Final Judgment.

Existentialism – the philosophical approach based on the idea that there is no difference between the external and internal world and that all existence is in the state of mind. Religious existentialism affirms that religious truth is to be found in religious experience itself.

Faith – the term has different meaning for Christians and Jews. The Hebrew word *emunah* denotes having confidence and trust in something or someone. This is the Jewish understanding of faith.

The Christian understanding is that faith is reliance on the death of Jesus, not one's good works, as well as trusting in God's promises as revealed in Scripture.

Flusser, David – twentieth-century Jewish scholar of early Christianity and the New Testament, who taught at the Hebrew University of Jerusalem.

Free will – the divinely given human capacity to make free choices for good or evil.

Fundamentalism – originally this word was used to describe a literal approach to reading Scripture. Today it is loosely used to denote exclusivist religious belief systems, and sometimes it is used to refer to those who wish to impose their views on others.

Garden of Eden – the location in which Adam was placed by God (Gen. 2:15) and where the first human family was established. The term is also used in Judaism as a synonym for Paradise, the heavenly abode.

Gentile – one of the nations. The term is used in the Bible to denote those who are not the children of Israel (i.e. the rest of the world).

Gospels – accounts of the ministry, death and resurrection of Jesus and commonly referred to as the first four books of the NEW TESTAMENT: Matthew, Mark, Luke and John.

Halachah – the corpus of Jewish religious law and practice.

Hassidism – the Jewish religious revivalist movement that emerged in the late eighteenth century in central and eastern Europe, which appealed to the less educated Jewish masses in particular. The movement was typified by ecstatic (mystical) devotion, personal spirituality and charismatic leadership. Today the term is often used (imprecisely) as synonymous with ultra-ORTHODOX.

Hebrew Bible – also referred to by the Hebrew acronym TaNaKh – i.e. Torah (Pentateuch), Nevi'im (Prophets), Khetuvim (Writings) – that make up the body of literature that Christians know as the Old Testament. Jews prefer not to use the term 'Old Testament' out of concern that this might reflect the ideas of REPLACEMENT THEOLOGY.

Hillel (the Elder) – Jewish sage of the first century BCE, probably the greatest scholar of his time; Pharasaic leader known for his compassion and tolerance. He founded the School of Hillel – the centre of learning that followed his orientation/teaching.

Holiness – God's essential nature (see Lev. 19:2), indicating that He is absolutely pure, clean and devoid of evil; the opposite of profane. It is a requirement of His people that they too be holy (e.g. Lev. 11:44).

Holocaust – the attempted extermination of the Jewish people by the Nazis and their collaborators during the period of World War II. The Nazis succeeded in murdering six million Jews, including a million and a half children.

Holy of Holies – the most sacred and innermost part of the Temple into which no one entered other than the High Priest on the holiest day of the year, the DAY OF ATONEMENT.

Infallibility of Scripture – the belief that all the books of the Bible were inspired by God and are absolutely true in all that they affirm.

Islam – the religion revealed to the Prophet Mohammed at the beginning of the seventh century in the Arabian peninsula, written down in the Quran (Koran).

Jerusalem – centrally located between the Dead Sea/River Jordan and the Mediterranean Sea and between the northern mountains of the Holy Land and the southern desert, it was a Jebusite stronghold until captured by David, who made it his capital, uniting the disparate tribes of Israel around it. Subsequently it was joined to a hill north of it on which the Temple was built and from where the city expanded to the west.

Jew – term used to identify the descendants of the children of Israel and thus synonymous with Israelites and Hebrews. However, its origins are from the name Judah (Jacob's fourth son) and the Roman form of the name, Judea. After the rule of Solomon, his kingdom split into two, the northern kingdom known as Israel and the southern as Judah (where the tribe of Judah was dominant). The tribes in the north were conquered and exiled by the Assyrians in the eighth century BCE and were assimilated into other populations (the ten lost tribes.) Thus only the tribes of Judah remained, and the names Judah and Israelite became synonymous.

Jewish mysticism – see KABBALAH.

Josephus (Flavius) – first-century Jewish military leader during the war against Rome; historian and major source of data regarding Second Temple Judaism; one of the chief representatives of Jewish–Hellenistic literature.

Judaism – the religion of the Jews.

Justification by faith – the Christian belief that one is declared righteous in God's sight by faith, not good works, the object of faith being Jesus Christ.

Kabbalah – sometimes used interchangeably with the term JEWISH MYSTICISM. However, the mystical search for union with God has always been part of Judaism. Kabbalah is the medieval esoteric system of knowledge that describes a mystical cosmology, i.e. explanation of how the world functions and is influenced.

Karaites – Jewish sect originating in the eighth century whose doctrine is chiefly characterised by its denial of Talmudic/ rabbinic tradition.

Land of Israel (Holy Land, Promised Land, Land of Canaan, Palestine) – name/s to denote the territory that the Bible describes as the divinely mandated homeland of the descendants of Abraham, Isaac and Jacob.

Law – an imprecise translation of the Hebrew word TORAH which is more correctly translated as 'instruction'.

Lord's Supper – also referred to as Holy Communion. The partaking of bread and wine which Jesus instituted with his disciples (Matt. 26:26–30) and continued by his followers to commemorate and partake in the body and blood of Jesus.

Luther, Martin – sixteenth-century PROTESTANT reformer who revived the teaching of JUSTIFICATION BY FAITH alone, but sadly also known for his anti-Semitic views.

LXX (Septuagint) – Septuagint is the Greek word for seventy and is used to refer to the Greek translation of the Hebrew Bible, traditionally attributed to seventy Jewish sages brought together for this purpose by Ptolemy in the third century BCE.

Maimonides (1135–1204) – Moses Maimonides (i.e. the son of Maimon) was the greatest Jewish scholar, philosopher and codifier of the Middle Ages. Born in Cordoba, Spain, he eventually settled in Cairo (Fostat), Egypt, where he served as physician to the Sultan.

Marcion – second-century Roman Christian who propounded the heresy that all Christian connection with the Hebrew Bible (the Old Testament) should be severed.

Messiah – the Hebrew word for a person anointed with oil as a sign of special status/role. The term is used in the Hebrew Bible in reference to a priest or king, and especially in prophecies of the restoration of the royal house of David. Christianity identifies this role with the redeeming sacrifice of Jesus who is thus called Christ (*Kristos*, Greek for 'anointed one').

Messianic Age – the biblical vision of an ideal religio-ethical society.

Messianic believers – usually used to denote Jews who believe that Jesus is the Messiah.

Midrash – the Jewish homiletical exposition of biblical texts.

The classical period of Midrashic works is parallel to the period of the TALMUD.

Mishnah – the first written compendium of the legal sections of the ORAL TORAH written down c.200 CE by Rabbi Judah the Prince.

Mitzvah – commandment; also used to mean a good deed.

Moral Law – those aspects of legislation that refer to morality, as opposed to those which refer to ritual or symbolism.

New Testament – the Christian succession to the Hebrew Bible (called Old Testament by Christians); twenty-seven books (beginning with the GOSPELS, containing the first history of the Church (Acts) and twenty letters, thirteen of which were written by Paul the Apostle.

Noahide Covenant – see COVENANT.

Nostra Aetate – the document issued in 1965 by the Second Vatican Ecumenical Council which rejected the idea of Jewish guilt for the death of Jesus, both at the time as well as thereafter; affirmed the eternity of the divine Covenant with the Jewish people; and condemned anti-Semitism. This document revolutionised Catholic teaching regarding Jews and Judaism.

Oral Torah (Oral Tradition) – see TORAH.

Original sin – the Christian belief that the sin of Adam and Eve in the Garden of Eden was transmitted to the entire human race; consequently people are born with a sinful nature and a propensity to commit sin.

Orthodox Judaism – Jews who call themselves Orthodox mean by this that they are committed to the body of Jewish practice/law (in Hebrew, *halachah*) which they believe to have divine authority. Therefore, while *halachah* has rules and method of application to address changing situations, the structure of *halachah* should not be changed. Orthodox Jews are most obviously distinguished from their Reform and even Conservative counterparts by the degree of meticulous observance of Jewish ritual practice, e.g. the dietary laws, the Sabbath and formal prayer three times a day. In Orthodox synagogues men and women sit separately and there is no Orthodox ordination of women as rabbis.

Palestine/Palestinians – after the Jewish rebellions against Rome in the first and second centuries, the Romans exiled much of the population and sought to eliminate vestiges of particular Jewish attachment to the land. In addition to replacing the name Jerusalem with Aelia Capitolina, they replaced the name Judea with the name Palestine (taken from the name Philistines, the ancient tribes that populated the southwest coastal region). Until the establishment of the modern state of Israel, all residents of the Holy Land were referred to as Palestinians. After the establishment of the state of Israel, the word 'Palestine' came to be used to denote only the Arab residents and in particular those in the West Bank and Gaza who seek an independent state by that name.

Passover – the spring festival that celebrates the Exodus of the children of Israel from Egypt (see Exod. 12:14–20); Christians believe that they continue the celebration of Passover through the LORD'S SUPPER.

Pentateuch – the Five Books of Moses (Genesis, Exodus, Leviticus, Numbers, Deuteronomy) also known as the WRITTEN TORAH, which traditional Judaism has taught were revealed by God to Moses at Mount Sinai after the children of Israel's Exodus from Egypt. Thus all the commandments contained in the Five Books (which according to Jewish tradition come to

613) are viewed by the tradition as having been revealed/ confirmed at Sinai (not just 'the Ten Commandments').

Pharisees – possibly first used to refer to a particular religiously devout sect, but came to be used to denote those Jews who followed the teachings of the ORAL TRADITION as well as the WRITTEN TRADITION, believing both to be of divine authority. They placed special emphasis on the study of the tradition and established schools of learning for this purpose. Central to their theology were the doctrines of free will, reward and punishment (Heaven and Hell), resurrection and the importance of prayer – virtually all of which were not shared by the Sadducees.

Pluralism – the idea that there is no one exclusive claim on truth. The word is now widely used interchangeably with the idea of freedom of religious worship and practice.

Prophets – persons chosen by God to bring His Word to the people.

Protestant – first used in 1529 at a meeting in Spier, Germany, the term is used to denote one who follows the form of Western Christianity that rejected (i.e. 'protested against') the absolute authority of the Roman Catholic Church and some of its teachings and practices.

Providence – God's overruling grace in the affairs of people.

Rabbi – literally 'master'. The word refers to one who has acquired advanced competency in Jewish learning and knowledge of the religious tradition. For most of the last two thousand years it has been used to denote one who has been examined and found proficient in the corpus of *halachah* (Jewish practice and custom) and competent to give religious rulings accordingly. Thus the role of a rabbi as a congregational leader in the Jewish community has always been an educational one and not a liturgical one. In modern times, especially in less educated Jewish communities, rabbis have assumed more liturgical prominence. However, a rabbi is *not* a priest and has no intercessory standing. Judaism teaches that all people are able to enjoy 'direct communication' with God.

Rabbi Akiva – see AKIVA.

Reform Judaism – also known as Progressive Judaism, this is the modern stream of the Jewish religion that rejects the concept of divine origin and authority of the written and oral TORAH, believing that an individual's personal autonomy overrides traditional religious law (*halachah*). The Reform movement made radical changes to Jewish liturgy and rejected ritual observances that were considered irrelevant and inappropriate for modern society. However, the principle of autonomy has led to a great diversity in this movement and in many cases a new return towards greater traditionalism may be observed. Reform Judaism was the first Jewish religious movement to ordain women for rabbinic leadership.

Reformed theology – the main teachings of John Calvin regarding sin, faith, predestination and the ATONEMENT of Jesus Christ.

Replacement theology – the idea that the Church has replaced the Jewish people as the recipient and beneficiary of divine biblical promise, i.e. the Church is the New Israel in place of the Old Israel, the Jews.

Righteousness – one of God's essential attributes (see HOLINESS); also the standard of behaviour required by God for all His people.

Rosenzweig, Franz (1886–1929) – German Jewish theologian who founded the independent house of Jewish learning (Lehrhaus). Author of *Star of Redemption*.

Sabbath – the divinely ordained day of rest on the seventh day of the week, to be kept as a holy day in remembrance of creation and the Exodus (see Exod. 20:8–12 and Deut. 5:12–15).

Sacrificial system – the order of religious devotion in the Temple involving the offering up of animal and/or vegetable donations.

Sadducees – the party among the Jewish people during the Second Temple period that was made up primarily of leading priestly and wealthy land-owning families. The Sadducees rejected the extensive Oral Tradition (see TORAH) of the PHARISEES. They also rejected the latter's approach that religious leadership in the community should be based on knowledge and piety rather than status of birth.

Salvation – the Jewish use of this concept generally refers to the deliverance of the Jewish people from its enemies, the restoration of the exiles to the land (that would also be accompanied by the reconstruction of the Temple and the re-establishment of the Davidic kingdom) and the ushering in of an era of universal peace (see MESSIANIC AGE). The Christian view is that one is saved from sin and its penalty through faith in Jesus Christ (see JUSTIFICATION BY FAITH).

Saving faith – the Christian view that faith renders one righteous before God as opposed to a general faith in God without trust in Jesus.

Second Coming – the Christian teaching that the same Jesus who died and rose from the dead will come a second time – that the fulfilment of the messianic prophecies in the Hebrew Bible (and New Testament) concerning universal peace, etc., would then be ultimately achieved.

Second Temple – the Temple in Jerusalem reconstructed on

Mount Moriah on the site on which Solomon's Temple, the First Temple, stood before being destroyed by the Babylonians in the year 586 BCE. While the reconstruction of the Second Temple began at the end of the sixth century BCE, it only reached its full glory in the Hasmonean era (last two centuries BCE) and especially under the rule of Herod the Great.

Second Temple Judaism – a term used to describe the diverse expressions of Jewish life in the last centuries BCE and the majority of the first century CE, prior to the destruction of the Second Temple by the Romans in the year 70 CE.

Sephardi(c) – the term is commonly used (though imprecisely) to describe Jews from Muslim lands, or more specifically those who follow specific customs and liturgical rites accepted in those lands. The word actually means 'Spanish', reflecting the degree to which Jews from the Iberian peninsula settled in North Africa, Asia Minor and the Middle East after their expulsion at the end of the fifteenth century. However, Sephardic communities also existed in Christian Europe both before and after the expulsion from Iberia.

Septuagint – see LXX.

Sermon on the Mount – Jesus' best-known sermon (Matt. 5–7) in which he unveiled his view of the Torah (especially the Decalogue) and contrasted it with the narrower interpretation of other Jewish authorities of his time.

Shabbat – see SABBATH.

Shabbat meal – on Friday night and Saturday during the day, festive meals celebrate the Sabbath with food, drink, study and song, giving thanks to the Creator and Guide of the Universe.

Shammai – Jewish scholar who lived in the first century BCE, usually referred to in the context of debate with his contemporary, HILLEL. Generally Shammai takes a stricter line/ interpretation than Hillel. Similarly to the latter, he established a school (the School of Shammai) that followed his approach.

Simon Bar Cuziba – see BAR COCHBA.

Sin – failure to do the right thing/live the right way in accordance with God's commandments or will.

Sinai Covenant – see COVENANT.

Stendahl, Bishop Krister – former Presiding Bishop of the Church of Sweden and former Dean of the Harvard Divinity School.

Strack, Hermann – nineteenth-century German scholar of New Testament and rabbinic literature.

Supercessionism – see REPLACEMENT THEOLOGY.

Tabernacle – while the term is used in reference to the Sanctuary that housed the Ark of the Covenant, it is also used to describe the booth that Jews construct for the Harvest Ingathering Festival (the Festival of Tabernacles) in keeping with Leviticus 23:39–43.

Talmud – the Talmud is basically the exposition of the MISHNAH. However, the Talmud contains not only the discussions in the schools of learning of the religious legal aspects of Jewish tradition (*halachah*) but also homiletical exposition and legends (*aggadah*). There are two Talmuds, the Jerusalem (or Palestinian) Talmud (often referred to by the letters TJ) that records the discussions in the schools in the land of Israel until around the end of the fourth century CE; and the Babylonian Talmud (referred to by the letters TB), the record of the stronger and longer-lasting study centres in Babylon. Accordingly the Babylonian Talmud, written down around the year 500 CE and divided into thirty-six tractates (i.e. separate books; some are referred to in this work, e.g. TB Sanhedrin), is the principal and more extensive text serving as the main point of reference for the CODES and rabbinic ruling.

Targum/s – literally, 'translation/s'. The word refers to the Aramaic translations of the Books of the Bible. Often in translating the text, the Targums expounded and in effect commentated on it.

Temple (Temple Mount) – the Sanctuary built for the service of God on Mount Moriah (Mount Zion) in Jerusalem.

Ten Commandments – another name for the Decalogue in Exodus 20 and Deuteronomy 5.

Tertullian (155–230 CE) – church leader and prolific Christian author who lived in Carthage, North Africa.

Tetragrammaton – Greek for 'a four-lettered word' and refers to the four-lettered Hebrew name for God, YHWH.

Torah – literally 'instruction'. Torah usually refers to the Written Torah, i.e. the Five Books of Moses (PENTATEUCH). It is also sometimes used to describe Judaism as a whole, thus including the Oral Torah (Oral Tradition) which refers to the body of clarification and exposition of the Written Torah, as well as additional traditions which, according to Orthodox teaching, go back to the revelation at Mount Sinai (essentially contained in the TALMUD). Traditional Judaism has therefore taught that the Oral Torah as well as the Written Torah has divine authority.

Trinity – the teaching of the Christian Church, both Protestant and Catholic, that God is one and yet revealed in three Persons, Father, Son and Holy Spirit.

Triumphalism – the tendency to fall into arrogant pride because of a conviction that the triumph of one's own person or one's own religious group is certain.

Ultra-Orthodox Judaism – ultra-Orthodoxy (sometimes referred to as 'fervently Orthodox') refers to those within Jewish Orthodoxy who seek to live in maximal isolation from non-Jewish culture and see modernity as a cultural threat. They tend either to wear clothing from a few centuries ago and/or dress in black and white clothing.

Universalists – those who believe that all people will be 'saved', regardless of their belief or conduct.

Vicarious atonement – the view that an animal sacrifice takes the place of sinners by which the debt of sin is cancelled. Christianity teaches that this was done when Jesus died on the Cross for the sins of the world.

Whitehouse, O.C. – late nineteenth/early twentieth century British Bible scholar.

Written Torah – see PENTATEUCH.

Yad Hachazakah – Maimonides' codification of the corpus of *halachah*, Jewish practice.

Yahweh (God the Redeemer) – the name of God which was given meaning at the time of the Exodus. See TETRAGRAMMATON

Zealots – the Jewish religious nationalists who led the rebellion against the Romans in the seventh decade of the first century CE that led as a consequence to the destruction of the Temple.

Zionism – the name given to the political movement that originated in the late nineteenth century with the purpose of restoring Jewish national sovereignty in the ancestral biblical land of the Jewish people.

General index

Biblical index

Hebrew Bible (or Old Testament)